CONTEMPORARY GERMAN WRITERS

SARAH KIRSCH

Series Editor

Rhys W. Williams has been Professor of German and Head of the German Department at University of Wales Swansea since 1984. He has published extensively on the literature of German Expressionism and on the post-war novel. He is Director of the Centre for Contemporary German Literature at University of Wales Swansea.

CONTEMPORARY GERMAN WRITERS

Series Editor: Rhys W. Williams

SARAH KIRSCH

edited by

Mererid Hopwood and David Basker

CARDIFF
UNIVERSITY OF WALES PRESS
1997

© The Contributors, 1997

British Library Cataloguing-in-Publication Data
A catalogue record for this book is available from the British Library.

ISBN 0–7083–1336–1

Cover design by Olwen Fowler.
Typeset at the Department of German, University of Wales Swansea.
Printed in Great Britain by Dinefwr Press, Llandybïe.

Contents

List of Contributors

Heinz Ludwig Arnold is editor-in-chief both of the journal *Text + Kritik* and the *Kritisches Lexikon zur deutschsprachigen Gegenwarts- literatur*. He has published extensively on post-war German litera- ture (especially on Dürrenmatt) and is a personal friend of Sarah Kirsch. He was visiting academic at the Centre for Contemporary German Literature in Swansea in 1995.

Anthony Bushell is Professor of German at the University of Wales, Bangor. His study *The Emergence of West German Poetry from the Second World War*, appeared in 1989. He has also published articles on Kaschnitz and Kunert.

Michael Butler is Professor of German and Head of Department at the University of Birmingham. He has written extensively on twentieth-century German literature, in particular on the work of Frisch and Dürrenmatt. His essay 'Der sanfte Mut der Melan- cholie. Zur Liebeslyrik Sarah Kirschs' appeared in 1989.

Mererid Hopwood is Lecturer in German at the University of Wales Swansea. Her study *Johann Peter Hebel and the Rhetoric of Orality* was published in 1994. She has written on the work of Rose Ausländer and has translated Welsh poetry into German. She is co-ordinator of the Centre for Contemporary German Literature.

Martin Kane is Reader in German at the University of Kent at Canterbury. His *Weimar Germany and the Limits of Political Art. A Study of the Work of George Grosz and Ernst Toller* appeared in 1987. He has published extensively on the literature of German Expres- sionism and on post-war writing, in particular on the writing of the former GDR.

Günter Kunert belongs to the group of former GDR writers who moved to the West after the Wolf Biermann expulsion. After a successful career in the GDR – he was awarded the Heinrich Mann Prize in 1962 and the Johannes R. Becher Prize in 1973 – he made an equally successful transition to the Federal Republic, winning the Heinrich Heine Prize in 1985 and the Friedrich Hölderlin Prize in 1991. Kunert's highly individual vision, expressed in both poetry and volumes of short prose, offers private resistance to social pressures, a kind of psychological 'Abtötungsverfahren' (the title of a poetry volume of 1980). Kunert, a personal friend of Sarah Kirsch, shares her fondness for the landscape of Schleswig-Holstein.

Rhys W. Williams is Professor of German at the University of Wales Swansea and Director of the Centre for Contemporary German Literature. He has published extensively on German Expressionism (Sternheim, Benn, Carl Einstein and Toller) and on contemporary literature (Andersch, Böll, Siegfried Lenz, Martin Walser and Peter Schneider).

Preface

Contemporary German Writers

Each volume of the Contemporary German Writers series is devoted to an author who has spent a period as Visiting Writer at the Centre for Contemporary German Literature in the Department of German at the University of Wales Swansea. The first chapter in each volume contains an original, previously unpublished piece by the writer concerned; the second consists of a biographical sketch, outlining the main events of the author's life and setting the works in context, particularly for the non-specialist or general reader. A third chapter will, in each case, contain an interview with the author, normally conducted during the writer's stay in Swansea. Subsequent chapters will contain contributions by invited British and German academics and critics on aspects of the writer's *œuvre*. While each volume will seek to provide both an overview of the author and some detailed analysis of individual works, the nature of that critical engagement will inevitably depend on the relative importance of the author concerned and on the amount of critical material which his or her work has previously inspired. Each volume includes an extensive bibliography designed to fill any gaps or remedy deficiencies in existing bibliographies. The intention is to produce in each case a book which will serve both as an introduction to the writer concerned and as a resource for specialists in contemporary German literature.

Sarah Kirsch

The current volume opens with five new texts by Sarah Kirsch, texts inspired by her stay in Swansea; these poems, together with three poems from *Erlkönigs Tochter* stimulated by a previous visit to Swansea, form the raw material of Mererid Hopwood's detailed analysis in Chapter Eight. After a brief biographical sketch and an interview with Sarah Kirsch we include a short, previously unpublished, tribute by Günter Kunert, a tribute which throws almost as much light on Kunert's own experience as on that of

Kirsch herself. Martin Kane's contribution concentrates on Kirsch's poetry written in the former GDR and offers analysis of her gradual transition from a social and political vision acceptable to the authorities to a more subjective vision, viewed with suspicion by the state. Kane takes his analysis up to the publication of *Drachensteigen*, the first volume to appear in the West after Kirsch's *Umzug*. While Anthony Bushell covers a similar range of early poetry, he concentrates not on the political implications of Kirsch's writing in the GDR but on poetic structures and thematic implications, on the 'struggle between cohesion and energy' in both her poetry and, interestingly, in her watercolours. In electing to concentrate on Kirsch's prose writings, Michael Butler brings the survey of Kirsch's work up to date, since she has shown a predilection for prose forms in the last decade. His analysis concentrates on the balance in her writing between affirmation and morbidity, between happiness and a sense of loss. What Butler refers to as 'teasing ambiguities' in Kirsch's prose is confirmed and further exemplified by Rhys W. Williams's detailed analysis of *Das simple Leben*. This chapter, together with Mererid Hopwood's examination of very recent (and seemingly very private) poetic utterances, concentrate on Kirsch's work of the 1990s. The final article in the volume is Heinz Ludwig Arnold's personal reminiscence about Kirsch, a counterpoint to Kunert's contribution with which the book begins. As in previous volumes of the series, the book concludes with an exhaustive bibliography. The Centre for Contemporary German Literature is particularly pleased that the publication of this volume coincides with the award to Sarah Kirsch of the Büchner Prize.

Abbreviations

Full bibliographical details appear in Chapter Eleven.

The following abbreviations refer to the editions stated in brackets after the titles and are valid for each of the chapters in this volume unless otherwise stated.

A	*Allerlei-Rauh. Eine Chronik* (1988)
B	*Bodenlos* (1996)
D	*Drachensteigen* (1979)
Ei	*Eisland* (1992)
E	*Erdreich* (1982)
ET	*Erlkönigs Tochter* (1992)
GS	*Gespräch mit dem Saurier* (1965)
I	*Irrstern. Prosa* (1986)
K	*Katzenleben* (1984)
Kk	*Katzenkopfpflaster* (1978)
L	*Landaufenthalt* (1969)
Lw	*Landwege* (1985)
LP	*La Pagerie* (1980)
R	*Rückenwind* (1977)
S	*Spreu* (1991)
SL	*Das simple Leben* (1994)
Sch	*Schwingrasen. Prosa* (1991)
Z	*Zaubersprüche* (1972–3)

1

Fünf Gedichte

SARAH KIRSCH

Caswell Bay

Der Sternfisch der Limpet erwarten

In dunklen Höhlen rettende Flut.

Verändert schwebst du

Rauchend über die Klippen ich bin

Dein Schatte blaue Hyazinthen

Hinter den Ohren

Seestück

Ich bin die

Mutter der auf dem

Meer segelnden

Söhne warte am

Strand mit den

Zündhölzern in der

Schürzentasche.

Auflaufendes Wasser Vollmond

Wo er geht am Strand von Mumbles ich

Seh es da ich ihm folge schon seit zwei Leben

Wolfssiegel tiefeingeprägt Krallen ich suche

Neun Arten Wolfsmilch die sonnenwendige die

Kreuzblättrige niederliegende die

Mandelförmige das Bingelkraut Zypressen-

Ruten- und Meerwolfsmilch jene bitttre

Euphorbia austriaca daß er nicht in

Fallgruben stürzt wenn der Mond abnimmt

In den Wellen

Das Meer so

Grün und so offen

Habe die Füße

Im Wasser

In den Wellen

Sehe ich Fische

Der Sommer der

Sommer ist da

Bei dir.

Gwyll

Dein Gesicht schöner als Wollgras als

Knabenkraut draußen im Moor.

Dein flatterndes Haar gleich

Wenn die Sonne hinter dem Fluß

Aufgeht oder der erste Sonnenstrahl

Auf deiner Wange

(Gwyll = gälisch Zwielicht)

2

Sarah Kirsch:
Outline Biography

MERERID HOPWOOD

1935	Born, Ingrid Bernstein, in Limlingerode (Southern Harz, GDR), on 16 April, daughter of a telephone engineer. Brought up in Halberstadt.
1958	Married Rainer Kirsch.
1959	Graduated in Biology from Halle University with a dissertation entitled: 'Über Ektoparasiten bei Muriden in und in der Umgebung von Halle'.
1963–5	Attended the *Johannes R. Becher Institut für Literatur* in Leipzig.
1965	Publication of her first volume of poetry, *Gespräch mit dem Saurier*, written jointly with Rainer Kirsch. The volume was awarded the *Kunstpreis der Stadt Halle*.
1967	Publication of her second volume of poetry, *Landaufenthalt*.
1968	Free-lance writer in East Berlin. Divorced from Rainer Kirsch. Relationship with the poet Karl Mickel, father of her only son Moritz (born 1969). Kirsch was finally given a one-and-a-half room flat on the seventeenth floor of a block in Prenzlauer Berg (Fischerinsel 9). She lived on meagre earnings from translations.
1969	Attack on the poem 'Schwarze Bohnen' at the Sixth Writers' Congress in East Berlin.
1973	Publication of *Die Pantherfrau. Fünf unfrisierte Erzählungen aus dem Kassetten-Recorder*. This year also saw the publication of *Die ungeheuren bergehohen Wellen auf See* and the volume of poetry *Zaubersprüche*. She was awarded the *Heinrich-Heine-Preis der DDR*.
1976	*Rückenwind* appeared, and Sarah Kirsch was awarded the *Petrarca-Preis*. This year also saw the beginning of a

four-year relationship with the West German poet Christoph Meckel. In November she was a signatory of the letter protesting against the expulsion of Wolf Biermann from the GDR. In December her membership of the SED was revoked.

1977   After facing severe reprisals for being a signatory of the Biermann letter, Kirsch's request for an exit visa was granted. She left East Berlin on 28 August 1977, moving in the first instance to West Berlin.

1978   Kirsch was awarded the *Villa-Massimo* Scholarship; she spent six months in Rome, where she met the composer Wolfgang von Schweinitz.

1979   *Drachensteigen,* the first volume of poetry to include poems written in the West, appeared.

1980   *La Pagerie,* a volume of poetic prose evoking her encounter with the Provençal landscape, was published.

1981   Kirsch was awarded the Austrian State Prize for Literature and the *Kritikerpreis.* She moved to a village near Bremen.

1982   Publication of *Erdreich.*

1983   Kirsch moved to the former school house in Tielenhemme, in the Dithmarschen area of Schleswig-Holstein where she still lives. She was awarded the *Roswitha-Gedenkmedaille* of the town of Bad Gandersheim.

1984   *Katzenleben* was published and Kirsch was awarded the *Friedrich-Hölderlin Preis* in Bad Homburg.

1986   Kirsch was awarded the *Weinpreis der Literatur.*

1987   Publication of *Irrstern.*

1988   *Allerlei-Rauh* appeared and Kirsch was awarded the *Kunstpreis des Landes Schleswig-Holstein* and the *Stadtschreiber-Literaturpreis* of the city of Mainz.

1989   *Schneewärme* published. First visit to the Department of German, University of Wales Swansea.

1991   *Spreu* and *Schwingrasen,* two prose volumes, published.

1992   *Erlkönigs Tochter* appeared.

1993   Kirsch was awarded the *Kulturpreis der Konrad-Adenauer-Stiftung.*

1994   *Das simple Leben* published; second visit to Swansea as guest of the Centre for Contemporary German Literature in the Department of German.

1995   *Ich Crusoe* published. Kirsch vehemently opposed the unification of the PEN Club of the Federal Republic and that of the former GDR.

1996   *Bodenlos* published; Sarah Kirsch awarded the *Georg-Büchner-Preis*, the first woman to receive the prize since Christa Wolf sixteen years earlier. Kirsch appointed to the Brothers Grimm Professorship at the University of Kassel.

1997   Kirsch awarded the *Annette-von-Droste-Hülshoff-Preis*.

3

Fragen hinter der Tür:
Gespräch mit Sarah Kirsch

MERERID HOPWOOD UND ANNETTE ZIMMERMANN

MH/AZ: Sie erhielten bereits mehrere literarische Preise, darunter den Petrarca-Preis und den Hölderlin-Preis. Nun hat man Ihnen den Büchner-Preis verliehen. Wie war Ihre erste Reaktion, als Sie diese Nachricht erhielten?

SK: Überraschung.

MH/AZ: Was halten Sie generell von der Vergabe literarischer Preise?

SK: Sie sind notwendig, da das Einkommen oftmals gering ist. Sie sind ein Glücksfall, denn es gibt auf diesem Gebiet nie nirgendwo dies: Gerechtigkeit. Es gibt sehr gute Schriftsteller, die so gut wie nie Beachtung finden bei den eitlen prestigesüchtigen Mitgliedern einer Jury.

MH/AZ: Das letzte Mal, das eine Frau den Büchner-Preis erhielt, war vor 16 Jahren; damals ging er an Christa Wolf. In Großbritannien hat man vor dem Hintergrund der Tatsache, daß solche Preise in der Regel an Männer gehen, die Konsequenzen gezogen und den *Orange-Prize* eingeführt, der ausschließlich an Schriftstellerinnen verliehen wird. Sie haben sich früher gegen eine solche Sonderbehandlung von Frauen im Literaturbetrieb ausgesprochen. Wie stehen Sie heute dazu?

SK: Ein Preis der nur an Frauen verliehen wird, würde mich nicht besonders erfreuen. Ausgrenzungen sind Diskriminierungen. Gründe dafür kann ich nicht anerkennen.

MH/AZ: Politische Interpretationen Ihrer Werke haben Sie manchmal mit Verwunderung zur Kenntnis genommen und sich von Sozialismus und Feminismus eher distanziert. Kann man denn aufgrund des herausragenden Stellenwertes, den Natur und Landschaft in Ihren Gedichten haben, auf ein Bekenntnis zu 'grünem' Gedankengut schließen?

SK: Die Lage des Blauen Planeten ist so katastrophal, daß es auf Veränderungen menschlichen Verhaltens in knapper Zeit ankommt, nicht auf Parteibücher.

MH/AZ: Lassen Sie uns noch einmal auf die Bedeutung der Landschaft in Ihrer Lyrik zurückkommen: Inwiefern ist sie Quelle Ihrer Inspiration, inwiefern Medium für Ihren Schaffensprozeß? Ist sie im Sinne der Romantik eine Reflexion des Ich oder aber wirkt sie auf das Ich ein und motiviert zum Schreiben?

SK: Die Natur ist die Kulisse für innere Befindlichkeiten und reizt durch ihr Wechselspiel zu erforschenden Aufzeichnungen, naturwissenschaftliches Interesse führt auch die Feder, Vergleiche der wiederholten irdischen Erscheinungen drängen sich auf. Künstler sind Experimentatoren auf allen Gebieten.

MH/AZ: Viele Ihrer Kollegen und Kolleginnen behaupten, nur zu Hause schreiben zu können. Bei Ihnen scheint das Gegenteil der Fall zu sein. Stimmt das so?

SK: Ja, es fällt mir an vielen Orten etwas ein oder zu.

MH/AZ: Viele Ihrer Gedichte und Prosastücke der letzten Jahre beschäftigen sich mit fremden Ländern. Könnte man dennoch soweit gehen und behaupten, daß das Reisen letztendlich mehr über das Selbst, über das Menschliche an sich enthüllt als über die besuchten Orte?

SK: Die oftmals fremden Orte sind hervorragende Punkte, an denen man seine Gedankenfäden, das Spinnengarn Ende des Sommers festzurren kann.

MH/AZ: Bei der Lektüre Ihrer neueren Gedichte läßt sich feststellen, daß Sie ihnen eine sehr persönliche Note verliehen haben. So tauchen beispielsweise Namen von vermutlich real existierenden Personen auf, Sie nehmen Bezug auf spezifische Örtlichkeiten und Begebenheiten, die ja dem Großteil der Leser verborgen bleiben müssen. Haben Sie diesen Weg bewußt eingeschlagen? Wie glauben Sie, gehen Leser mit solchen 'Rätseln' um?

SK: Auch ein Rätsel kann schön sein.

MH/AZ: Seit einigen Jahren sind Sie dazu übergegangen, auch Aquarelle zu veröffentlichen. Welche Bedeutung hat das Malen neben dem Schreiben fur Sie?

SK: Ein meditativer Ausgleich. Dilettantismus im schönsten Sinne.

MH/AZ: Welche literarische Vorbilder haben Sie? Seit Ihrem ersten Besuch in Swansea 1992 läßt sich unschwer der Einfluß von Dylan Thomas erkennen . . .

SK: Keine. Mitunter benutze ich stilistische Zitate.

MH/AZ: Das literarische Milieu eines jeden Landes ist meist relativ begrenzt; jeder kennt jeden. Welchen Einfluß hat diese Tatsache auf Ihr Schreiben?

SK: Das literarische Milieu, das mich beeinflussen kann, ist weder geographisch noch zeitlich begrenzt. Gryphius oder Jan Skacel oder Robert Walser oder die Frau Sappho können die Nächsten sein, an die man sich wendet.

MH/AZ: Der Stil Ihrer Werke hat sich im Laufe der Zeit gewandelt, er hat fragmentarische nahezu notizenhafte Züge angenommen; Sie verzichten weitgehend auf Interpunktion, die eigenwillige Grammatik ist gerade zu Ihrem Markenzeichen geworden. Wie kam es zu dieser Entwicklung?

SK: Die Schreibart kann sich im nächsten Moment wieder auf längere Stücke dehnen. Man darf nicht darauf schließen, daß alles bis zum Verschwinden kürzer wird. Fehlende Interpunktion gibt auch Freiheit. Macht mehrere Lesarten oft möglich. Auch die Grammatik ist Ausdruck der Seele.

4

Zu Sarah Kirsch

GÜNTER KUNERT

Jene Geheimpolizei, die in der einstigen DDR die Dichter über-
wachte und ausforschte, bezeichnete letztere als «Operative Vor-
gänge» und verlieh jedem einzelnen einen Decknamen. So wurde
ich zum OV «Zyniker», andere erhielten abwertendere Epitheta,
und nur Sarah Kirsch, wie sich nach dem Öffnen der Akten er-
wies, wurde durch ihren Decknamen nicht herabwürdigt. Man
nannte sie mit einem vogelkundlichen Gattungsbegriff nahezu
poetisch «Milan».

Der Milan, Sammelbezeichnung für unterschiedliche Erschein-
ungsformen der Gabelweihe, ist ein Geschöpf, von dem es heißt,
er flöge mit weitgespreizten, langgezogenen Schwingen traumhaft
leicht durch die Lüfte. Mir scheint, da hat ein Geheimpolizist in
einem ungewöhnlichen Anfall von Intuition für Sarah Kirsch das
entsprechende Analogen gefunden. Einzelgängerisch wie der
Milan, mit scheinbarer Leichtigkeit sich über die Erde erhebend
und ihr doch zugehörig – das trifft auf die Dichterin unbedingt
zu.

Sie ist, um ein Wort aus der Ornithologie zu gebrauchen,
«standorttreu». Denn sie kehrt nach allen Ausflügen in die Welt
immer wieder an ihren Platz in der Abgelegenheit zurück, in die
Einsamkeit und Stille nördlicher Ländlichkeit. Hier ist der Himmel
fast grenzenlos, ein Trost für alle jene, deren Dasein einstmals von
tatsächlichen Grenzen eingeengt gewesen ist, und ein immer
wiederkehrender Anlaß, sich der eigenen Freiheit schreibend zu
vergewissern.

5

'. . . aus der ersten Hälfte meines Landes':[1] Sarah Kirsch in the GDR

MARTIN KANE

One scarcely needs to be reminded that Sarah Kirsch was one of a new generation of young GDR poets who, in the sixties, were credited with resuscitating for the East German lyric the primacy of subjective feeling, and, as one critic has put it, contributing to 'die Rehabilitierung der Sinnlichkeit'.[2] This was an uncertain accolade, explicable only against a background of poetic energies channelled, in the first decade or so of the founding of the GDR, into eulogies to the new state. For poets such as Becher, Weinert and Kuba, communists returning from exile who wished to see their vision of the future made reality in 'diesem besseren Lande',[3] an uncritical *Volksverbundenheit* and *Parteilichkeit* were the order of the day. Becher's 'Der Staat',[4] Kuba's 'Dem 7. Oktober 1949',[5] and Erich Weinert's 'Bekenntnis eines Künstlers zur neuen Welt'[6] – to offer typical examples – are all uncritical, and somewhat premature celebrations of the new order. Even if the daily reality of the GDR did not always fulfil the expectations and hopes of this older generation, nothing resembling reservation is ever allowed to surface in their poetry. A notable exception here of course is Bertolt Brecht (one thinks of the *Buchower Elegien* with their reflections on the shadow still cast by the Nazi past, and on the events of 17 June 1953, which came as an enormous shock to him).

Not that the young Sarah Kirsch herself was not enamoured of the goals and ideals of the new state in the making. In a frank interview with Klaus Wagenbach just two years after she moved to West Berlin, she makes no bones about the unalloyed commitment to the GDR which she had felt as a teenager. She speaks of being part of something purposeful and on the move ('Ich hatte den Nachkrieg gesehen, und es war ja Jahr für Jahr wirklich aufwärts gegangen'), and above all, it was fun.[7] It was only when 'Erwartungen stoßen sich an der Prosa des Lebens' (Hans Kaufmann, in an essay which sets Kirsch's poetry among the 'besten künstlerischen Leistungen unserer Literatur')[8] that the illusions would crumble. As she herself would put it in the poem 'Besinnung':

> Was bin ich für ein vollkommener weißgesichtiger Clown
> Am Anfang war meine Natur sorglos und fröhlich
> Aber was ich gesehen habe zog mir den Mund
> in Richtung der Füße. (Z, 43)

Sarah Kirsch's first collection of poetry, *Gespräch mit dem Saurier*, authored jointly with her then husband Rainer Kirsch, had a mixed reception. How what now appears a somewhat guileless collection might be transformed into a political football is demonstrated by its West German reviewer Sabine Brandt who facetiously compared the Kirschs to the Kilius/Baumler ice skating duo, describing them as 'das Schau-Paar der jungen Zonenlyrik' who had prospered only as the result of the 'erzieherische Hilfe der Partei'.[9] In retaliation, Klaus Höpcke used his notorious attack on Wolf Biermann (*Neues Deutschland*, 5 December 1965) to toss a brickbat back at the *Frankfurter Allgemeine Zeitung* for its treatment of two of the GDR's rising stars too.[10] In her review, Brandt had characterized Kirsch as a poet who 'sich naiv-verspielt [gibt], sie plappert [. . .] oder sie träumt', but seemed more concerned to deliver a few rather cheap jibes than to substantiate her critical reservations. Nevertheless, it is difficult to regard Sarah Kirsch's contributions to *Gespräch mit dem Saurier* as the work of a writer who would become 'die bedeutendste deutschsprachige Dichterin der Gegenwart'.[11] She herself later came to see these poems as something of an embarrassment, implicitly endorsing Adolf Endler's negative view of them: 'Es gab Zeiten, wo er meine Gedichte als *baby-talk* bezeichnete. Der kluge Endler ist ein scharfsinniger Kritiker, man kann von ihm lernen.'[12]

Kirsch is perhaps a little too dismissive. Many of these early poems are admittedly marred by a skittish sentimentality:

> Guten Tag, Kamm!
> Willst du
> nicht bei mir bleiben,
> daß ich immer schön bin?

Guten Tag, Katze!
Willst du
nicht bei mir bleiben?
Du bist lustig,
tanzt auf zwei Beinen.

Guten Tag, Lieber!
Willst du
nicht bei mir bleiben?
Ich bin schön
und kann lachen. ('Bekanntschaft', *GS*, 6)

They also seem uncertain about their audience. Ronald Paris's cover and accompanying illustrations, along with poems such as 'Känguruh und Laus' or 'Liebes Pferd', would not be out of place in a book for children:

Liebes Pferd,
es ist verkehrt
zu sagen,
es sänke dein Wert
durch elektrifizierte Lieferwagen.

Du Pferd brauchst nicht zu weinen
und dich auch nicht zu schämen;
es kommen gute Zeiten:
Meine Enkel werden mit deinen
morgens,
bevor sie eine Rakete nehmen,
ein Stündchen um den Startplatz reiten. (*GS*, 31)

There is however a greater substance in some of the poems here – 'Hierzulande' (*GS*, 26–7) a feisty resistance, in insect imagery, to collective norms and values, or the ecological poems 'Bootsfahrt' and 'Die Stadt' (*GS*, 17 and 18) – quite apart from that sensuous restlessness which one has come to associate with Sarah Kirsch's mature poetry. In 'Kleine Adresse' for instance, it leans over-heavily on Mayakovsky for its articulation, and relies too much for its own good on politically acceptable shibboleths:

Aufstehn möcht ich, fortgehn und sehn,
ach, wär ich Vogel, Fluß oder Eisenbahn,
besichtigen möcht ich den Umbruch der Welt.

Wo ist die Praxis hinter der Grenze? Wo
Steppenkombinate? Slums? Streiks?
Weizen im Meer? (*GS*, 37)

Nevertheless, in its will to break out – formally and thematically –
a poem such as this indicates that the door of the kindergarten is
open, and that Sarah Kirsch is ready to begin writing verse for
grown-ups.

Despite this, one could not have anticipated the extent of the
liberation from 'baby-talk' which *Landaufenthalt* of 1967 with its
establishment of a singular and original poetic identity would
represent. The comments of Heinz Czechowski in 1991 suggest
that she was opening up entirely new ground, and not only for
herself:

> Ihr erster eigener Gedichtband *Landaufenthalt* bestätigte nur noch, was
> ihre Freunde und Leser schon wussten: Mit Sarahs Gedichten war ein
> neuer, bisher ungehörter Ton in der deutschen Lyrik zu hören.[13]

Czechowski does not say precisely what is so innovative, but we
note immediately, in comparing the first poem of the new volume,
'Der Wels ein Fisch der am Grund lebt', with 'Kleine Adresse', the
last poem of her half of *Gespräch mit dem Saurier*, that the
'Plapperton' has gone,[14] along with the childlike rhymes which
generated it. Both poems are clearly sparked by the claustrophobic
travel restrictions felt not just by poets but by all GDR citizens at
this time; both reflect a yearning to escape and experience a wider
world. Yet how different the rendering of this is in the two
poems. In 'Kleine Adresse' the globetrotting vision had been
launched on the cliché of the weary, desk-bound writer and
wrapped in an utterly awkward metaphor ('Ach, warum bin ich
Dichter, ackre den Wagen / der Schreibmaschine übers kleine
Papierfeld [. . .]' [*GS*, 38]). In 'Der Wels' Kirsch exploits her
knowledge of biology to deliver a startling image of a
sand-hugging fish whose body shape evokes the plane in which
the poet immediately finds herself soaring up and away. There is
brief homage to ideological expectations:

> [. . .] da
> werden Demonstrationen gemacht weiß
> werden die Transparente getragen mit schwarzer Schrift
> gegen Schlächterei Ungleichheit Dummheit (*L*, 5)

but what seems most to excite is the experience of listening to wildly disparate forms of music while in the air: 'ich höre Bach und Josephine Baker das ist ein Paar' (*L*, 5). This is the climax of the poem. Unlike in 'Kleine Adresse', there is no reference to returning to the GDR.

In *Landaufenthalt*, the virtual abandonment of rhyme, and a much more adventurous use of elliptical narrative and enjambement, punctuation and syntax (the eccentric orthography of her later work, poetry and prose, is not yet a feature), may be seen as an act of self-assertiveness. It is matched by the emergence of an increasingly rebellious poetic personality, at times, as in 'Aufforderung', 'ein Maultier das störrisch ist' (*L*, 25); at others, 'ein Tiger im Regen' – a bundle of anarchic energy rampaging through East Berlin finally to implode on its own sense of isolation and frustration ('Trauriger Tag', *L*, 10).

What is the relationship in *Landaufenthalt* of this uncomfortable lyrical persona to the GDR and the wider political world? If love and nature poems loom large in this volume, they are always made to yield social and historical perspectives. Like Brecht, who claimed to be driven to his desk only by the 'Reden des Anstreichers', but could still find time to rejoice in the 'grünen Boote und die lustigen Segel des Sundes',[15] Kirsch manages to hold the balance between celebration of the natural world, exploration of feelings and emotions, and the call of history. In 'Fahrt II', what begins as appreciation of the delights of railway journeys 'durch mein kleines wärmendes Land' ends as sombre comment on the irreconcilable differences between the two German states:

> Die Fahrt wird schneller dem Rand meines Lands zu
> ich komme dem Meer entgegen den Bergen oder
> nur ritzendem Draht der durch Wald zieht, dahinter
> sprechen die Menschen wohl meine Sprache, kennen
> die Klagen des Gryphius wie ich
> haben die gleichen Bilder im Fernsehgerät
> doch die Worte
> die sie hörn die sie lesen, die gleichen Bilder
> werden den meinen entgegen sein. (*L*, 6-7)

The Gryphius reference demonstrates that Kirsch is well aware of the wider turbulence of German history, past and present. The comment that the same words and images in East and West are open to vastly different ideological interpretations reminds us that her understanding of these darker chapters has its roots in the particular *Geschichtsverständnis* of the GDR. If, however, we look at those poems in *Landaufenthalt* which approach the legacy of the recent German past, as well as those which have something to say on contemporary issues such as the Vietnam war, we see emerging an independent view which has worked itself free of orthodoxy and any element of *Auftrag*. Consider, for instance, the opening two stanzas of 'Hirtenlied':

> Ich sitz über Deutschlands weißem Schnee
> der Himmel ist aufgeschlitzt
> Wintersamen
> kommt auf mich wenn nichts Schlimmres
> Haar wird zum Helm
> Die Flöte splittert am Mund
>
> Der Wald steht schwarz es kriecht
> Draht übern Felsen es riecht
> nach Brand da hüte ich
> die vier Elemente am Rand des Lands. (*L*, 18)

The poet, surveying in isolation the frozen, ominous landscape of a divided Germany, finds images which can only evoke past destruction ('es riecht / nach Brand') and present strife ('es kriecht / Draht übern Felsen'), or anticipate some approaching Armageddon ('Haar wird zum Helm'), in a world – surely an echo of Adorno's Auschwitz comment here – in which art can no longer function ('die Flöte splittert am Mund').

In 'Der Schnee liegt schwarz in meiner Stadt' (*L*, 20) she once again sets herself apart from the generality. While her fellow human beings are 'um diese Zeit / auf ihrem breiten Chaiselongue / und essen warmes Brot' (signals of comfortable, complacent indifference?), she is walking abroad 'im schwarzen Pelz', her alienation and troubled awareness reflected in distorted perception of sights and sounds ('Der Schnee liegt schwarz', 'Tauben brüllen'). Her only communicants are dogs 'voll Schlamm und Rauch' (to be equated perhaps with the 'findige[n] Tiere' in Rilke's first *Duino Elegy*?), who direct her to the 'weißen Schnee / der auf dem Judenfriedhof ist'. We are left wondering. 'Judenfriedhof' is far too resonant a term to be merely dropped into the topography of the poem, and yet Kirsch refuses to allow it to yield up any easy holocaust clichés. Is the whiteness of the snow, in a town where elsewhere it has been turned to black mush, a clue? Here in the Jewish cemetery it is pristine, untouched by the churning imprint of curious, concerned visitors. The cemetery has been forgotten – along with the fate of the descendants of those buried there, Jews who did not have the privilege of dying, as Kirsch puts it elsewhere, 'gewaltlos'[16] – by those snug and oblivious to everything but their warm loaves.

The perspective in these two quite different 'German' poems is aggressively idiosyncratic, the one springing from a deep historical pessimism, the other – as does Jurek Becker's *Jakob der Lügner* – defying orthodox GDR reading of the fateful Jewish dimension of the recent past. Her poetry on the subject of Vietnam holds fewer surprises, being unmistakably the work of someone who, as co-editor of the documentary work *Vietnam in dieser Stunde*,[17] was quite clearly partisan. Daily images of the Vietnam war were an inescapable feature of the years in which *Landaufenthalt* was being written, and it is unsurprising that it should often disrupt the narrative of poems of quite other preoccupation. The richly erotic celebration of summer as a lover's attentiveness in 'Süß langt der Sommer ins Fenster', for instance, is brutally arrested by the sudden intrusion of one of the grimmest and best-remembered images of the Vietnam war – children fleeing with napalm burns down a country road:

> [. . .] ach gerne
> höb ich den Blick nicht aus seinem Blau
> wären nicht hinter mir die Geschwister
> mit Minen und Phosphor (*L*, 50).

Kirsch's most usual poetic strategy is to allow political or historical concerns to arise unexpectedly and indirectly out of an intensely personal experience. Rarely are they tackled head-on. The longer narrative poems 'Der Milchmann Schäuffele' (*L*, 46) and 'Legende über Lilja' (*L*, 30) – painstaking recreations of single tragic fates, victims of pogrom and holocaust – as well as the three poems she addresses specifically to the Vietnam war are the exception. Given her ideological sympathies, Hans Wagener's observation about the first of them, 'Bevor die Sonne aufgeht', that the poet 'sich ausdrücklich [. . .] mit den Vietkong solidarisch [erklärt], indem sie sie mehrfach als ihre Brüder apostrophiert',[18]

would not seem to be problematical. Yet this interpretation makes
certain aspects of the poem strangely incongruous. Why the mention of a 'Hickorybaum'? Why are the 'brothers' depicted as deer
hunters (associations are immediately triggered with the film *The
Deer Hunter)*? Why are we told 'sie haben die neusten Gewehre
gehn außer Lands sie sollen schießen wenn ein Mensch im Visier
ist'? All this invites us to think of American country-boy con-
scripts rather than the Vietcong. This is surely not due to clumsy
choice of reference and setting on Kirsch's part. What Wagener
has failed to observe is that she has adopted three quite separate
lyrical voices for her triptych, a different one for each of the three
poems. Here in the first, that of the sister of the young American
soldiers to be; in the second that of Vietnamese peasants watching
an enemy plane come down: '[. . .] ach wie ihre Fenster blitzten
und die Zahlen / auf den Flügeln, eh sie in die Palmen fielen
[. . .]' (L, 28); and in the third a voice identical with her own
which anticipates the end of the war and the moment when the
aggressors 'falln / ein Schwarm Fliegen, mit ihren Flugzeugen,
Schiffen, Kanonen / zurück in ihr Land'(L, 29).

Kirsch's poetry of the sixties has to be seen in the context of
debates about poets who had been born in the 1930s, grown up in
the GDR, and whose motivation for writing was, as Günther
Deicke points out in a sympathetic essay on Volker Braun, quite
different from that of his own generation:

> [. . .] wo wir uns noch vornehmlich mit der Vergangenheit
> auseinandersetzten, fanden sie in dieser ihrer Gegenwart bereits ihre
> Reibungsflächen, entdeckten, wo wir Fortschritt sahen, schon
> Unvollkommenheiten, sie griffen ein, stritten sich mit ihresgleichen
> und Gleichgesinnten und demonstrierten in der Praxis, was wir erst
> mühsam theoretisch begreifen mußten: die Schärfe und Härte und
> Lösbarkeit der nicht antagonistischen Konflikte.[19]

In his 'Versuch über Versuche junger Lyriker' Hans Richter is
much less sympathetic, criticizing this new breed of poet for
retreating into 'eine menschenarme oder menschenleere Natur',
and inclining to the treatment of 'denkbar kleine Themen' – all of
which he attributes to having lost 'die nötige Sicherheit des Urteils
in den vorrangigen politischen Fragen'.[20]

He was not alone in failing to see that the more modest *Gestus*
in the work of this younger generation was an attempt to make
sense of a personal reality in a society which stressed the social

collective, and resulted from having 'auf den Realitäten bestanden [. . .] gegenüber Wunschvorstellungen und Illusionen'.[21] Christian Löser's review of two anthologies by relatively unknown GDR poets, *Saison für Lyrik. Neue Gedichte von siebzehn Autoren,* (Aufbau, 1968), and *auswahl 68. Neue Lyrik – Neue Namen,* published by the Verlag Junges Leben,[22] was typical of the critical reserve which these fresh linguistic and thematic impulses provoked in more conservative quarters. Löser maintained that too many of the poems in *Saison für Lyrik* were characterized by 'Züge der Distanziertheit, von understatement, von verfremdeter Haltung zur Wirklichkeit'. His response to the poems by Sarah Kirsch in the volume was similarly cool. The 'lyrisches Ich' in 'Grünes Land', he complained, offered 'keine *realen* Wirkungsmöglichkeiten'; there were 'Züge des Fatalismus' in 'Der Himmel auf tönernen Füßen'; and 'Weites Haus' was little more than 'ein vage formulierter Wunsch statt des Blicks auf notwendiges kollektives Handeln'.

This was literary criticism reduced to evaluating a line of verse by its ability to be socialist and up-beat, an approach replicated at the *VI. Schriftstellerkongreß* of 1969 in the mood of general disapproval directed at recent developments in the lyric. Max Walter Schulz in his opening speech chose to damn with faint praise:

> Die Lyrik, soweit sie sich nicht in Scheinproblematik, in falschen Bildern vom Sozialismus und in intellektualistischen Lamentos gefällt, gestaltete ihr lyrisches Subjekt aus neuen verläßlichen Objekten,[23]

continuing with a diatribe against Reiner Kunze whose *Sensible Wege* had been published, without proper East German authorization, by Rowohlt in March of that year:

> Es ist alles in allem [. . .] der nackte, vergnatzte, bei aller Sensibilität aktionslüsterne Individualismus, der aus dieser Innenwelt herausschaut und schon mit dem Antikommunismus, mit der böswilligen Verzerrung des DDR-Bildes kollaboriert [. . .]. (*VI.,* 53–4)[24]

As Adolf Endler reminds us in an article on the impoverished response of GDR *Germanistik*, and Hans Richter in particular, to new developments in the lyric, Sarah Kirsch had also been under attack. He quotes the invective directed at her by *Neues Deutschland*:

Sarah Kirsch fühlt sich unverstanden, glaubt darum, sich durch törichte Bemerkungen, die sie wohl für witzig hält, und durch kaum dechiffrierbare Gedichte, deren schwankende, durchgehende skeptische Haltung aber doch offensichtlich wird, interessant zu machen.[25]

Günther Deicke added to this chorus of disapprobation with his comments at the *VI. Schriftstellerkongreß* on Sarah Kirsch's 'Schwarze Bohnen':

Wir wollen nicht ungerecht sein: Die Verlorenheit in diesem Gedicht ist tief poetisch. Aber sie kennzeichnet eine spätbürgerliche Position der Aussichtslosigkeit jeglichen Beginnens. Jeder von uns kennt solche Stimmungen [. . .] Aber gestaltenswert, scheint mir, ist erst ihre Überwindung, das erst macht uns zu sozialistischen Poeten (*VI.*, 231–2).

Thus might the sledgehammer of ideology be used to crack a poetic nut which seemed to be a highly original, but entirely harmless registration of the response of a woman waiting in vain for her faithless lover. Interestingly enough, this poem would receive a second airing at the *VII. Schriftstellerkongreß* four years later when Karl-Heinz Jakobs used it in his advocacy of a literature which was more complex in its treatment of socialist realities. Poems such as 'Schwarze Bohnen', he maintained, 'die uns zunächst fremd erscheinen', deserved a much wider audience: 'auch diese Gedichte müssen unters Volk gebracht werden. Und auch diese Gedichte müssen in ihrer ganzen Tiefe begriffen werden.'[26]

In the seventies Sarah Kirsch was the GDR's foremost woman poet and also the author of two significant prose works – *Die ungeheuren bergehohen Wellen auf See*, seven stories (nine in the edition published in Zurich in 1987), and *Die Pantherfrau*, a collection of lightly edited interviews with five women from different stations in GDR life.[27] Coming as it does some four years before Maxie Wander's *Guten Morgen, du Schöne*, and despite Kirsch's reservations about the work,[28] *Die Pantherfrau* must be seen as a pioneering contribution to *Frauenliteratur* in the GDR. What links all but one of the five women interviewed here (ironically, the exception is the one happiest in her personal life) is the success they have made of their professional careers. All are models for what women might attain in a state which, for all that its constitution vouchsafed, was dominated by patriarchal values. Since the

collapse of the GDR, Kirsch's demand, in her '8 Nachbemer-
kungen' to the volume, that 'Der Schriftsteller muß Chronist seiner
Zeit sein' seems more valid than ever. In emphasizing 'die
unterschiedlichen Sprechstrukturen der 5 hier versammelten
Frauen', she has preserved some of the codes – now vanished – by
which the individual in the GDR articulated her/his loyalty to the
ideological and social system. Significantly, the two women closest
to the centre of power – the *Genossin* from the 1930s who worked
her way up through the *Aufbau* years to a high position in the
Ministry of Culture, and the historian turned local politician – are
the least spontaneous in their language and expression. In both
cases, the authentic edge captured in the free flow of the individual interviews with the panther tamer, the housewife and the
working mother, tends – as they become aware of the exemplary
dimension to their lives – to disappear behind official register and
phraseology. Here lies one of the many merits of *Die Pantherfrau* –
its reminder of that particular brand of discourse for public consumption which kept the majority of the East German population
in a permanent state of schizophrenia.

Although they are described as 'Erzählungen', Sarah Kirsch
claims, tongue in cheek, that all the pieces in *Die ungeheuren
bergehohen Wellen auf See* 'sind ihr irgendwo wirklich passiert oder
begegnet [. . .] so skurril manches auch klingen mag, wovon sie
[. . .] berichtet'.[29] As in *Die Pantherfrau,* she tests the official version of how women lived in the GDR against the reality of their
lives. In 'Merkwürdiges Beispiel weiblicher Entschlossenheit' the
inescapable problem of *Doppelbelastung* in the GDR is explored
from an unusual angle, as a model worker, having failed to per-
suade a colleague to father a child by her (a purely business
arrangement), adopts one instead, only to find her reputation for
dedication at work under threat as she begins to put child before
job. In the commissioned story which provided the title for Edith
Anderson's collection of sex change stories by various hands, *Blitz
aus heiterm Himmel,*[30] the female narrator discovers she is able to
play a much fuller part in her partner's life after she is changed
into a man and becomes a pal, rather than the part-time lover and
housekeeper she has been hitherto – a bizarre perspective on
stereotyped and inflexible gender roles in the GDR.

These two stories, along with *Die Pantherfrau,* throw fascinating
light on the situation of women in the GDR. None the less, it is in
her poetry that the essence of Kirsch's particular contribution to

GDR women's writing is to be found. She is at her most distinctive in her nature or love poetry, not infrequently, as we noted
with 'Süß langt der Sommer ins Fenster', combining the two. From
her earliest poems on, we find Kirsch in the role of insecure and
vulnerable partner whose capacity to feel and love without
reserve is seldom fully reciprocated. This seems to remain a constant of all her love poetry. It is the way, however, in which her
ability to work through that insecurity and vulnerability matures
and develops which delivers the heightened impact of her later
poems. In *Gespräch mit dem Saurier* the response to the threat of
rejection moves barely beyond juvenile coquettishness:

> Du willst jetzt gehen?
> Das sag ich dem Mond!
> Da hat sich der Mond
> im Großen Wagen verladen,
> der fühlt mit mir, weißzahnig
> rollt er hinter dir her!
> ('Dreistufige Drohung', *GS*, 7)

In *Landaufenthalt*, the persona has become much more resilient.
She has equipped herself with a self-irony which, while not pro-
hibiting meticulous examination of feelings of anxiety and loss,
helps to discipline and control them.[31] In 'Bei den weißen
Stiefmütterchen', for instance, a suggestion of distancing humour
is evoked in the communication of her tangle of fears and emotions to a willow tree:

> im Park wie ers mir auftrug
> stehe ich unter der Weide
> ungekämmte Alte blattlos
> siehst du sagt sie er kommt nicht
>
> Ach sage ich er hat sich den Fuß gebrochen
> eine Gräte verschluckt, eine Straße
> wurde plötzlich verlegt oder
> er kann seiner Frau nicht entkommen
> viele Dinge hindern uns Menschen. (*L*, 11)

This ability to ironize gently not only her own position, but also
that of an errant lover is seen to further good effect in 'Don Juan
kommt am Vormittag' (*Z*, 48) when her West Berlin 'Freund-

bruder'[32] arrives for their rendezvous with flapping coat and on a racing bike (as Franz Fühmann puts it: 'Variation über ein Thema von Mozart: eine Mythengestalt im tiefsten Herunterge-kommensein').[33]

It is in *Zaubersprüche*, however, that we find the most intense and poetically precise focus on her emotional life, and her most powerful love poetry. Love here is many different things. It can be a beckoning siren: 'Nebel zieht auf, das Wetter schlägt um. Der Mond versammelt Wolken im Kreis. Das Eis auf dem See hat Risse und reibt sich. Komm über den See' (Z, 5). It can be sheer physical, erotic pleasure: 'Verdammt! Wir haben Glück gehabt gerade in einem Bett' (Z, 64), 'Ich werd dich jetzt das wird aber gut sein' (Z, 46). Most often, however, it can bring the pain of loss or betrayal. But pain is always a source of energy. Kirsch never languishes in the role of neglected, forsaken lover. In the final section of *Zaubersprüche*, 'Katzenkopfpflaster', she seeks to bewitch and bind, or even reject, the fickle object of her affections with a series of full-blooded, and blood-curdling, incantatory appeals to the elements:

> Phöbus rotkrachende Wolkenwand
> Schwimm
> Ihm unters Lid vermenge dich
> Mit meinen Haaren
> Binden ihn daß er nicht weiß
> Ob Montag ob Freitag ist. (Z, 47);

> Frost Regen und Schlamm über die Füße dir
> Zarthäutiger, Eis dir zwischen die Zehen mit denen ich
> Einstmals die Finger verflocht, du schiebst sie
> Nicht mir untern Tisch. (Z, 50);

> Eu Regen Schnee Gewitter Hagelschlangen
> Steigt aus des Meeres bodenloser Brut
> Und haltet euch in Lüften eng umfangen
> Bis er auf meinem roten Sofa ruht. (Z, 51)

Arguably her most exciting love poem is 'Ich wollte meinen König töten', a controlled torrent of contradictory emotions, intentions and desires triggered, the poem implies, by a lover in whom she feels deceived:

Ich wollte meinen König töten
Und wieder frei sein. Das Armband
Das er mir gab, den einen schönen Namen
Legte ich ab und warf die Worte
Weg die ich gemacht hatte: Vergleiche
Für seine Augen die Stimme die Zunge
Ich baute leergetrunkene Flaschen auf
Füllte Explosives ein – das sollte ihn
Für immer verjagen. (Z, 8)

It is hard to understand this poem as being about the difficulties of writing 'unterm Zwang der marxistischen Ästhetik'.[34] Surely the 'König' from whom she wishes to liberate herself, whom she by turns wants to kill, malign, damage, and betray – and from which, ultimately, 'Das Ding Seele dies bourgeoise Stück' holds her back – is a 'König des Herzens' rather than a 'König des Staates'? These are terms used by Kirsch in a cycle of poems which resulted from a stay in the early 1970s at Schloß Wiepersdorf, at that point an *Erholungsheim* for GDR writers. The cycle explored, *inter alia*, her feelings of affinity for Bettina von Arnim who lived in Wiepersdorf from 1814 to 1816 and is buried in the local church. One poem in particular is of relevance here:

Dieser Abend, Bettina, es ist
Alles beim alten. Immer
Sind wir allein, wenn wir den Königen schreiben
Denen des Herzens und jenen
Des Staats. Und noch
Erschrickt unser Herz
Wenn auf der anderen Seite des Hauses
Ein Wagen zu hören ist. (R, 27)

Interpretations of the last three lines which detected a reference to the *Stasi*, have, perforce, to see the 'Königen des Staates' as implying in some way Kirsch's involvement with the state and its possible baleful repercussions. This was discounted by Kirsch herself in a discussion with Berlin schoolchildren. It was *Der Spiegel* which, in the wake of the Biermann affair, had seen the car as a 'Stasi-Auto'. She had intended the incident to be understood in the context of a broken relationship:

Das habe ich so geschrieben, als ob man da in einem Haus sitzt. Man hat sich von irgend jemand getrennt, lebt jetzt dort und erschrickt doch noch, wenn man das Auto hört und denkt, jetzt kommt er.[35]

In fact the reference here to writing to the 'Königen des Staats' must apply to Bettina and her study of mass poverty in Prussia which she dedicated to Wilhelm IV in 1843: 'Dies Buch gehört dem König'. Kirsch's concerns surely are with the 'Königen des Herzens'.

Many of Kirsch's love poems take us into territory shaped by fantasy and elements of magical incantation. But not all of her attempts to fathom an emotional life, which seldom seems to run smoothly, move in a world created by Kirsch, the 'approbierte Hexe'.[36] Nor, indeed, does it reveal itself at first glance as love poetry. In 'Still stürzen Wände ein', oblique statement and pathetic fallacy are deployed to give booming resonance to the passage of private calamity – here the unspecified bad news brought with the mail – in an indifferent world:

> Still stürzen Wände ein, der Apfelbaum fällt
> Mit roten Früchten ins Gras.
> Auf verbeulten Rädern jagen
> Kinder die Felder ab und die Postfrau
> Wäscht ihre Hände in Unschuld. (*R*, 52)

Only knowledge of what is most likely to shatter Kirsch's equilibrium enables us to speculate that the letter is a lover's rejection. Is it from Brecht again, one wonders, that she has learnt the laconic precision with which inner turmoil is rendered here, or the finding in nature of objective correlatives for emotional states? The process whereby Brecht, in 'Böser Morgen',[37] conveyed feelings of guilt and ambivalence by transforming a 'Silberpappel, eine ortsbekannte Schönheit' into 'eine alte Vettel', a lake into a 'Lache Abwaschwasser', and making fuchsias 'billig und eitel', is precisely mirrored here in images of walls collapsing and laden apple trees tumbling into the grass.

Sarah Kirsch is an uneasy ally of feminism. Answering a question on the subject of female emancipation put to her by a West German interviewer in 1978 she commented:

Da wird ja übertrieben bis sonst wohin. Buchläden, zu denen Männer keinen Zutritt haben, finde ich albern. Zu Lesungen, bei denen nur Frauen lesen und diskutieren, würde ich nie hingehen.[38]

And yet her love poetry which grapples so precisely and honestly with what she has felt and experienced as a woman, and in which – despite being so often the loser – she seems to emerge stronger and profounder, are eloquent testimony to the toughness and independence of spirit sought by the modern woman.

From the debates we have observed surrounding Kirsch's work in the 1960s it is clear that she would never be easily accommodated within the cultural orthodoxies of the GDR. Her youthful enthusiasm for the state gradually transformed itself into an attitude which Gerhard Wolf saw summarized perfectly in the opening lines of 'Tilia cordata', a poem written in the very late sixties:[39] 'Langsam nach Jahren geh ich / Vom Sein des Hunds in das der Katze' (*R*, 8). Familiarity with the ways of dogs and cats, with their very different kinds of loyalty to master or mistress, gives the key here to how Sarah Kirsch saw the changing nature of her relationship to authority in the GDR.

Zaubersprüche contained poems written in a spirit of uninhibitedness which arguably never expected to see the light of day and only did so as a consequence of Honecker's 'no taboos' speech of December 1972. The volume was none the less criticized for its predominantly pessimistic note, but found a powerful advocate in Franz Fühmann ('Was soll es, [. . .] daß man diesem zauberhaften Buch also Schwermütigkeit vorwirft und durch diese Denunziation bereits die Kritik geleistet glaubt?').[40] At the *VII. Schriftstellerkongreß* of November 1973 he administered a powerful rebuttal of the simple-minded argument that literature merely had to propose certain desirable (from an official point of view) circumstances for them immediately to become reality. Crisply scathing of those who had criticized *Zaubersprüche*, he dismissed the notion that it was the function of the writer to provide good cheer and morale boosters for the social process. This was to ignore or misapprehend the nature of the writer's craft: 'Wunschdenken', he noted, 'so gut es auch immer gemeint sei, bringt Gesellschaft wie Literatur nicht weiter.'[41]

Despite Fühmann's support, later consolidated in an eloquent examination of *Zaubersprüche* in *Sinn und Form*,[42] the volume signalled a further worsening of Kirsch's relationship with the cultural authorities. The five cryptic lines of 'Keiner hat mich verlassen' give her reaction to the ubiquitous *Bevormundung* of a state which measured its own present virtues against the tyrannies of the past, saw them in terms of what it magnanimously desisted from imposing on its citizens, rather than in terms of what it did to encourage them to take wing and flourish. If one is looking for signals which would take Sarah Kirsch to the point where she could say, 'in der DDR hätte ich nicht mehr schreiben können',[43] one can certainly be found in this poem:

> Keiner hat mich verlassen
> Keiner ein Haus mir gezeigt
> Keiner einen Stein aufgehoben
> Erschlagen wollte mich keiner
> Alle reden mir zu. (Z, 14)

All of this was only a prelude to the final break with the SED, precipitated by the Wolf Biermann affair when she was one of the twelve initial signatories to the petition in November 1976 against his expatriation. Put under pressure to withdraw her signature, she refused. Exclusion from the governing committee of the East Berlin section of the *Schriftstellerverband* and the Party soon followed. The publication of *Rückenwind* in December 1976 was greeted with deafening silence, the beginning of a campaign of intimidation in which she was put under surveillance by the *Stasi* and harassed by her neighbours. 'Juden heraus' was daubed on her door, and the notice board of the house on the *Fischerinsel* in East Berlin decorated with the message, 'Die Dame vom 17. Stock soll gefälligst ausziehen'.[44] Lines written in a very different context some years before now seemed to be prophetic of her present situation: 'Ich weiche ab und kann mich den Gesetzen / Die hierorts walten länger nicht ergeben' (Z, 52). Her application to leave the GDR was accepted with alacrity by the East German authorities, and at the end of August 1977 she moved to West Berlin.

A short explanatory note on *Drachensteigen* – the volume which bridges her move from the GDR to 'Wolfsland' (R, 33) – informs us that it consists of work produced between 1976 and the beginning of 1979 in the GDR, West Berlin and Italy. We are told that 'Der Rest des Fadens', the tenth of forty poems in all, was the first to be written in West Berlin. It is characteristic of the poems which draw on her exile in offering no easy statement on the troubling switch to entirely new social and political circumstances: 'Uns gehört der Rest des Fadens, / und daß wir dich kannten'(*D*, 16). Such is the final line of a poem ostensibly about kite-flying which, for the reader primed for a first reflection on expatriation, develops a tantalizing, enigmatically open image: a paper star ripped up into the light of an open sky, leaving nothing but broken string and a memory. Similarly, 'The Last of November', an impressionistic poem set in and around the weird waste land near the Reichstag in West Berlin, reserves its last lines for a mention of 'unsere toten Dichter' – her own fellow exiles, dead because they have been cut off from the roots of their own writing and the natural audience for it (*D*, 17).

This sense of loss and deracination hangs over the latter part of *Drachensteigen,* the poems written by Kirsch in Italy. It is moderated and kept from overwhelming her by a mystical feel for landscape and the total, euphoric embrace of moments delivered by the exotic shock of the Sirocco, and the light, weather and fauna and flora of the Mediterranean. But if this experience of the South sets in motion an almost metaphysical *frisson,* it is also a way of drawing sufficient breath to attempt to come to terms with recent emotional upheavals. She is not, in the contemplation of the very unprussian charms of Italy, above using them to ventilate ironic comment on her personal fortunes. As, for instance, in 'Dankbillett' when, sitting in Rome amidst fountains, *carabinieri,* and eucalyptus trees stirring in the breeze, she expresses mock gratitude to 'meinem vorletzten Staat' for having catapulted her into this casual paradise (*D*, 26).

If in other of these Italian poems the immersion in the rampant differentness of the country helps her to forget briefly the fact of emigration, it is clear that the pleasures grasped, and the consolations to be drawn from the intense experience of nature, are precarious. As in the poems in which a breathless account of domestic disorder renders the panic of separation from a lover ('Mir fällt alles aus der Hand, ich stürze / Über meine Füße [. . .]', *D*, 35), we sense the fragility of the poet's peace of mind. Happiness for Sarah Kirsch has always been an impermanent, elusive state, frequently a matter, as in 'Kiesel', of self-deception and a certain wilful disregard for what lies in wait:

> Ich gewöhn mich ins Glück. Der Fuhrmann
> Ohne Wagen und Pferd

Steht bis zum Hals im Fluß, gibt
Frohe Befehle. (*D*, 44)

Where does one existence end, and another begin? Sarah
Kirsch's subtitle 'aus der ersten Hälfte meines Landes' suggests a
deceptively clean break with the GDR. Looking at the gentle jab
she takes at former poet-friends in the cycle 'Reisezehrung' in
Erdreich (1982),[45] and *Allerlei-Rauh* (1988)[46] with its evocation of
Prenzlauer Berg and a summer in Mecklenburg, described vari-
ously as 'bezaubernd', 'verrückt', 'phantastisch' (her neighbour
Christa Wolf would also immortalize it in *Sommerstück*),[47] or con-
templating *Das simple Leben* (1994),[48] with its forays, real and in
the imagination, into the GDR, it is clear that Sarah Kirsch's preoccupation with her former home is a continuing one. The country,
its people and poets, are a stubbornly lingering presence which
weaves in and out of everything she has subsequently written.
The title of the essay which might grapple with all this would not
be 'Sarah Kirsch *in* the GDR', but 'Sarah Kirsch *and* the GDR' – a
much more complex proposition.

Notes

[1] See Sarah Kirsch, *Die ungeheuren bergehohen Wellen auf See.
Erzählungen aus der ersten Hälfte meines Landes* (Zurich, Manesse, 1987).
This is an extended version of *Die ungeheuren bergehohen Wellen auf See.
Erzählungen* (Berlin, Eulenspeigel, 1973). Abbreviations used in this article
refer to those listed on the abbreviations page, apart from Z which refers
to the 2nd extended edition of *Zaubersprüche* (Ebenhausen bei München,
Langewiesche-Brandt, 1974) and L which refers to the 1967 edition of
Landaufenthalte. Gedichte (Berlin and Weimar, Aufbau).
[2] Michael Franz, 'Zur Geschichte der DDR-Lyrik. 3. Teil: Wege zur
poetischen Konkretheit', *Weimarer Beiträge*, 15 (1969), 1204
[3] See Adolf Engler and Karl Mickel (eds.), *In diesem besseren Land.
Gedichte der Deutschen Demokratischen Republik seit 1945* (Halle/Saale,
Mitteldeutscher, 1965).
[4] Johannes R. Becher, 'Der Staat', *Gesammelte Werke*, vol. 6, *Gedichte
1949–1958* (Berlin and Weimar, Aufbau, 1973), 89.
[5] Kuba, 'Dem 7. Oktober 1949', in *Brot und Wein. Gedichte*, 2 edn.
(Leipzig, Reclam, 1975), 99–100.
[6] In Uwe Berger and Günther Deicke (eds.), *Lyrik der DDR* (Berlin and
Weimar, Aufbau, 1970), 33–44.
[7] 'Von der volkseigenen Idylle ins freie Land der Wölfe. Ein Gespräch
mit Sarah Kirsch', *Freibeuter*, No. 2 (1979), 85–93.

[8] Hans Kaufmann, 'Zur DDR-Literatur der siebziger Jahre', *Sinn und Form*, 30 (1978), 171–6, here 176 and 171.

[9] Sabine Brandt, 'Poetischer Paarlauf – Kur und Pflicht. Gedichte von Sarah und Rainer Kirsch aus Ostberlin', *Frankfurter Allgemeine Zeitung*, 17 July 1965.

[10] Klaus Höpcke, '. . . der nichts so fürchtet wie die Verantwortung. Über "Antrittsrede" und "Selbstporträt" eines Sängers', in Elimar Schubbe (ed.), *Dokumente zur Kunst-, Literatur-, und Kulturpolitik der SED* (Stuttgart, Seewald, 1972), 1065–9, here 1067.

[11] Jochen Hieber, 'Baumgefiederter Deich. Die Gedichte der Sarah Kirsch', *Frankfurter Allgemeine Zeitung*, 15 July 1989.

[12] Interview with Hans Ester and Dick van Stekelenburg in Amsterdam, 3 May 1979, in Sarah Kirsch, *Hundert Gedichte* (Ebenhausen bei München, Langewiesche-Brandt, 1985), 123–34, here 127.

[13] Heinz Czechowski, 'Das Wiedererscheinen Sarah Kirschs in der Menge', *Börsenblatt*, No. 97, 6 December 1991, 4221.

[14] Sabine Brandt, 'Ein Hauch von Puppenheim. Die Lyrikerin Sarah Kirsch', *Die Zeit*, 29 March 1968, 12 (literature section).

[15] Bertolt Brecht, 'Schlechte Zeit für Lyrik', in *Bertolt Brecht. Werke*, vol. 14, *Gedichte 4* (Berlin and Weimar, Aufbau, Frankfurt am Main, Suhrkamp, 1993), 432.

[16] See the lines 'Es waren Steine zum Gedächtnis alter Juden / Gewaltlos starben sie in dieser Stadt' in the poem 'Lithographie' (Z, 35).

[17] Sarah Kirsch *et al.* (eds.), *Vietnam in dieser Stunde. Dokumentation* (Halle, Mitteldeutscher, 1968).

[18] Hans Wagener, *Sarah Kirsch* (Berlin, Colloquium, 1989), 23.

[19] Günther Deicke, 'Auftritt einer neuen Generation', in Annie Voigtländer (ed.), *Liebes- und andere Erklärungen* (Berlin and Weimar, Aufbau, 1972), 36–42, here 36–7.

[20] Hans Richter, *Verse, Dichter, Wirklichkeiten. Aufsätze zur Lyrik* (Berlin and Weimar, Aufbau, 1970), 241–2.

[21] Adolf Endler, 'Sarah Kirsch und ihre Kritiker', *Sinn und Form*, 27 (1975), 142–70, here 160.

[22] In *Neue Deutsche Literatur*, 17 No. 7 (1969), 155–61.

[23] Max Walter Schulz, 'Das Neue und das Bleibende in unserer Literatur', in *VI. Deutscher Schriftstellerkongreß vom 28. bis 30. Mai 1969 in Berlin. Protokoll* (Berlin and Weimar, Aufbau, 1969), 23–59, here 24. Subsequent page references in text = VI.

[24] Other texts were also under attack of course: Christa Wolf's *Nachdenken über Christa T*, for being 'angetan, unsere Lebensbewußtheit zu bezweifeln, bewältigte Vergangenheit zu erschüttern, ein gebrochenes Verhältnis zum Hier und Heute und Morgen zu erzeugen' (VI, 53). All this provoked no doubt by Marcel Reich-Ranicki's review of the novel and his comment: 'Sagen wir klar, Christa T. stirbt an Leukaemie, aber sie leidet an der DDR' (VI, 55–6).

[25] Adolf Endler, 'Im Zeichen der Inkonsequenz', in Gisela Rüß (ed.), *Dokumente zur Kunst-, Literatur- und Kulturpolitik der SED 1971–1974* (Stuttgart, Seewald, 1976), 263–9, here 267.

[26] In *VII. Schriftstellerkongreß der Deutschen Demokratischen Republik. Protokoll* (Berlin and Weimar, Aufbau, 1974), 116.

[27] See note 1 above.

[28] In an interview she commented: 'Ich würde dieses Buch nicht zur Literatur zählen. Es ist ein Halbfabrikat, aber ein wichtiges'. See 'Den Himmel beschreiben. Ein Gespräch mit Sarah Kirsch', *Die Zeit*, 28 October 1977, 48 (literature section).

[29] In Gudrun Skulski, 'Im Spiegel eigenen Empfindens. Begegnung mit der Schriftstellerin Sarah Kirsch', *Neue Zeit* (DDR), 21 December 1974, 16.

[30] Edith Anderson (ed.), *Blitz aus heiterm Himmel* (Rostock, Hinstorff, 1975).

[31] See Irmtraud Gutschke's comment, 'Sarah Kirsch hat viel Sinn für [. . .] die Ironie, die vor Enttäuschungen bewahrt', in 'Im Hier-Sein ein Anderswo', *Neues Deutschland*, 20 July 1990, 9.

[32] The reference is to Christoph Meckel, 'Der Dichter M. im Grunewald' (18).

[33] Franz Fühmann, 'Vademecum für Leser von Zaubersprüchen', *Sinn und Form*, 27 (1975), 385–420, here 406.

[34] See Michael Butler, 'Der sanfte Mut der Melancholie. Zur Liebeslyrik Sarah Kirschs', in Heinz Ludwig Arnold (ed.), *Sarah Kirsch, Text + Kritik*, 101 (1989), 50–60, here 52.

[35] 'Ein Gespräch mit Schülern', in Sarah Kirsch, *Erklärung einiger Dinge* (Ebenhausen bei München, Langewiesche-Brandt, 1978), 5–51, here 11.

[36] Roland H. Wiegenstein, 'Approbierte Hexe, Sprechstunden nach Vereinbarung', *Merkur*, 31 No. 2 (1977), 178–84, here 184.

[37] In *Bertolt Brecht. Werke*, vol. 12, *Gedichte 2* (Berlin and Weimar, Aufbau, Frankfurt am Main, Suhrkamp, 1988), 310.

[38] '"In der DDR könnte ich nicht mehr schreiben". Plädoyer für eine persönliche und vielstimmige Literatur', interview with Mathias Schreiber, *Kölner Stadt-Anzeiger*, 17 January 1978.

[39] This rough date can be deduced from Gerhard Wolf's comment, in a volume of essays published in 1989, that Kirsch had written this poem 'vor bald zwei Jahrzenten'. See Gerhard Wolf, 'Ausschweifungen und Verwünschungen, Vorläufige Bemerkungen zu Motiven bei Sarah Kirsch', in Heinz Ludwig Arnold (ed.), *Sarah Kirsch, Text + Kritik*, 101 (1989), 13–28, here 26.

[40] Franz Fühmann, 'Literatur und Kritik', in *Essays, Gespräche, Aufsätze 1964–1981* (Rostock, Hinstorff, 1993), 68–81, here 72.

[41] Ibid., 79.

[42] See note 33 above.

[43] 'Ein Lyriker braucht den Mut, auch einmal schlechte Gedichte zu machen', interview with Hilde Domin, *Bücherpost*, No. 15, 14 April 1978.

[44] See Eckart Krumbholz, 'Made in GDR: Sarah Kirsch', *Sonntag*, 24 December 1989.

[45] Sarah Kirsch, *Erdreich. Gedichte*, 37–44, here 43.

[46] See Bibliography.

[47] Christa Wolf, *Sommerstück* (Berlin and Weimar, Aufbau, 1989).

[48] See Bibliography.

6

The Problem of Structure and Themes in Sarah Kirsch's Early Poetry: *Landaufenthalt, Zaubersprüche* and *Rückenwind*

ANTHONY BUSHELL

One of the standard reference works on natural history offers the following entry:

> One usually thinks of catfish as being a plump, barbed fish which lies on the bottom and becomes active only when seeking food [. . .] Because of their secretive life habits and dismal appearance it is no wonder that catfishes have given rise throughout history to all sorts of tales and fables. We know very little about their life.[1]

It was not out of character that Sarah Kirsch, poet by profession but also an academically qualified scientist, should be attracted to a creature of 'dismal appearance', taking material with ostensibly such little promise for poetic exploitation to open the West German edition of her first solo book of poetry, *Landaufenthalt*:

> Der Wels ein Fisch der am Grund lebt
> hat einen gewölbten Rücken der Kopf ist stumpf
> der Bauch flach er paßt sich dem Sand an
> der von den Wellen des Wassers gewalzt ist . . . (L, 5)[2]

What happens next in the verse exemplifies an essential element in Sarah Kirsch's poetic practice: the imagination takes an unlikely point of departure and, unencumbered by punctuation, soars, quite literally in the case of the poem 'Der Wels ein Fisch der am Grund lebt', to a new and unpredictable vantage point:

> von dieser Gestalt wähn ich mein Flugzeug
> das hoch über der Erde steht, aus seinem Fischbauch
> ins Riesge gewachsen laden noch Flügel
> stumpfwinklig in windzerblasene Wolken
> unter mir Wälder Nadel- und Laubgehölz

This leap of perspective from the bottom of the sea into the air and back down to the earth is matched by a leap of reason since nothing in the poem so far has quite prepared the reader for the conclusion of the poem some seventeen lines later: 'ich höre Bach und Josephine Baker das ist ein Paar'. This incongruous juxtaposition, which shuns and defies any notion of resolution but in its colloquial phrasing invites a response, demonstrates a further hallmark of Kirsch's earlier work and explains simultaneously the attraction, the idiosyncrasies and the difficulties that much of her work, and especially her early poetry, presents to readers.

Sarah Kirsch's reputation as a poet was secured through the appearance of three early volumes of poetry published in her thirties while she was still resident in the former German Democratic Republic. And if it is possible to attempt to locate, externally at least, unifying periods in her work then the volumes *Landaufenthalt* (1967), *Zaubersprüche* (1973) and *Rückenwind* (1976) suggest a distinct stage in the emergence of Sarah Kirsch's lyrical voice. These were works that were available to an East German audience whilst she was still in the country and which were reprinted in the Federal Republic relatively soon after their GDR appearance. The poems they contain all fall before the poet's decisive encounter with the landscapes of France and Italy and before certain themes were to come to dominate contemporary German literature, in particular ecology and the women's movement, to which, with varying degrees of accuracy, her poetry has been said to be indebted.

Despite the differences that prevent these three volumes from being regarded unreservedly as an unimpeded and organic development of a coherent poetic stance, they have much in common; there is within the poetry of all three collections an undiminished sense of unrest which finds expression in the subordinate clause that forms the final sentence of the poem 'Ende Mai' in *Rückenwind*:

> [. . .] Wenn mein Leib
> Meine nicht berechenbare Seele sich aus den Stäben
> Der Längen- und Breitengrade endlich befreit hat. (*R*, 41)

Here lies a way into Sarah Kirsch's poetic world, both in its thematic intent and in its underlying principles of construction: there is the ever present and perilous challenge to the accepted syntax of the German language, perilous because it pushes the reader's concept of the dividing line between the coherent and the incoherent to the limits; there is also a tangible sense of struggle, as the persona behind the poems seeks to emerge. The poet's wish to disentangle herself from the daily constraints that locate us all to a particular place, a desire to escape from the lines of longitude and latitude that fix us with suffocating exactness as if they were a mesh placed over us, belong to an impulse towards 'Lockerheit und Leichtigkeit' (to use Kirsch's own terms) which she holds to be a fundamental principle of her poetic nature and which, in part, she subsequently saw as a need that could no longer have been met had she remained in East Germany. Correspondingly, the heavy use of first person forms *ich, mir, mein*, already evident in the fragment quoted immediately above, saturates much of the poetry of these early volumes. The poetic personality has no sense of false modesty and there are very few devices inserted into the texts of the poetry to discourage the naïve belief on the part of the reader, a belief which would be misplaced in the context of many other modern poets, that the *Ich* of the poem is the unmediated voice of the poet herself. Only after many re-readings does the frequently fractured syntax of Kirsch's poetry begin to make sense, both revealing its meaning and convincing the reader that the form chosen is the appropriate vehicle for what Kirsch wishes to say.

The breathless quality projected by her poetry can, and frequently does, leave the reader wondering if the poet is in full control of her own utterances. A barely mastered chaos speaks out from many of the lines and is indeed acknowledged in one of her poems:

> Meine Worte gehorchen mir nicht
> Kaum hör ich sie wieder mein Himmel
> Dehnt sich will deinen erreichen
> Bald wird er zerspringen ich atme
> Schon kleine Züge mein Herzschlag
> Ist siebenfach geworden schickt unaufhörlich
> Und kaum verschlüsselte Botschaften aus . . . (R, 34)

The absence of punctuation and the disregard for structural and grammatical cohesion undoubtedly irritates on first reading, and may even lead some readers to discard Kirsch's poetry from a feeling of exasperation. The poems' structures may even cause readers on their initial encounter with her verse to fail to see that, as with the poem 'Meine Worte gehorchen mir nicht', they are being confronted with a love poem. Kirsch is, however, very conscious of her technique and what she wishes to achieve through it, as she stated in an interview given three years after the appearance of *Rückenwind*:

> Wenn ich manchmal sehr wenig Kommata oder sonstige Satzzeichen verwende, so ist das, als ob ich zeigen will, wie schnell der Text gelesen werden muß, so atemlos und ohne abzusetzen, damit jedes Wort die gleiche Wertigkeit bekommt und nach rechts und links übergreift, ich meine jetzt auch sinngemäß.[3]

This expectation placed upon the reader could be interpreted as an act of provocation on the part of the poet towards her readership, an insistence that existing reading habits be abandoned in favour of a new reading method yielding insights of which traditional syntactical discipline would be incapable.

The challenge of Kirsch's earlier poetry resides not merely in the apparently eclectic and frenetic movement between individual lines and imagery; her work also displays a disregard for other principles of poetic composition that have traditionally steered readers through even demanding constructions. Kirsch's poems in these books, unless they belong to the shorter evocations and incantations that are a special feature of the collection *Zaubersprüche*, lack a focal or turning point, or are without an underlying, and therefore unifying, structure suggesting a culmination of the poet's thought process. If they could be compared with musical structures, they would strike the reader as a series of snatched phrases, arresting and startling in themselves, but in many instances without a firm sense of a home key or of being *durchkomponiert*. The point is perhaps best made by contrasting her work with a poem from the work of one of the most accomplished woman poets of the generation before Kirsch, Marie Luise Kaschnitz. The latter's poem 'Notizen der Hoffnung' is taken from *Dein Schweigen – Meine Stimme*, a work that predates Kirsch's *Landaufenthalt* by only four years:

> Nicht zu vergessender Stein
> Der mir den Himmel aufriß
> Brunnentief über den Erlen

Nicht zu vergessender
Singender Pfiff
Aus dem Herzen des Reisigfeuers.
Nicht zu vergessendes Wiegen
Ast über Ast
Der Knaben im Buchsenskelett
Nicht zu vergessende Märzsonne
Ungebührliches Scheinen
Und purpurner Seidelbast
Tannenschonungversteckt
Blühend für keinen.[4]

The techniques, the very raw material, employed by Kaschnitz are remarkably close to those found in the early Kirsch: a minimum of punctuation, the absence of complete grammatical units, a range of nature vocabulary that displays a delight in, and a detailed knowledge of, many botanic forms (and evoking in the mind of the reader a line from Kirsch's *Landaufenthalt*: 'ich unterscheide Simsen und Seggen so viel Natur'). Even the tone of Kaschnitz's poem, idyllic and elegiac, is not that far from the dominant mood of much of Kirsch's early work, and the similarity is echoed in the ambiguity of the conclusion, 'Blühend für keinen', a line suggesting a degree of impersonality and detachment which stands in uneasy relationship to the poem's title and its promise of hope, which is rarely impersonal. Such contradictions of mood abound too in *Landaufenthalt*, *Zaubersprüche* and *Rückenwind*, yet for all these points in common the impression of the work of the two poets could not be more different, and that difference can be attributed to the compositional coherence that sustains a poem such as 'Notizen der Hoffnung', where each segment adds to the previous one to create an impression of order and development and showing, as so often in the poetry of Kaschnitz, a fine sense for muted cadence that adds to the harmony of the composition.

It is illuminating to contrast 'Notizen der Hoffnung' with a poem such as 'Ich' from *Zaubersprüche*:

Meine Haarspitzen schwimmen im Rotwein, mein Herz
Sprang – ein Ei im kochenden Wasser – urplötzlich
Auf und es fiel, sprang wieder, ich dachte
Wo du nun wärest, da flogen die Schwäne dieses
Und auch des anderen Spreearms schnell übern Himmel.
Das Morgenrot, das dezemberliche, Bote

Vielleicht frühen Schnees, hüllte sie ein und die Hälse
Verlockung, sich zu verknoten, sie stießen
Fast mit der Kirche zusammen. Ich stand
Auf eigenen Füßen, Proleten unter den Gliedern, ich hätte
Mir gern einen Bärn aufgeladen ein Zopf aufgebunden
Ein Pulverfaß aufm Feuer gehabt. (Z, 73)

The poem is driven forward – with great intensity – by the energy and range of its imagery and its vocabulary; the one constant element that remains, as mentioned earlier, is the repeated use of first person forms which occur six times within twelve lines in a poem that already uses the first person as its title. The appositions are as startling as they are disconcerting ('mein Herz / Sprang – ein Ei im kochenden Wasser'), the imagery is eclectic, ranging from the very particular and exactly located in space and time ('Spreearm' and 'dezemberlich'), to the slight suggestion of the surreal: 'Meine Haarspitzen schwimmen im Rotwein'; at the same time other words such as 'Prolet' and 'Pulverfaß' invite a political and allegorical reading, but Kirsch's poetry refuses stubbornly to be approached in a way appropriate, for instance, to the work of Peter Huchel. There is at a compositional level a self-indulgent wilfulness in her poetic constructions when set against those of Marie Luise Kaschnitz, betraying a lack of feeling for cadence and cadenza, and therefore unity, to be found in the verse of the older poet.

If comparisons with music show up the cohesion of a poet such as Kaschnitz, reference to modern art may help illuminate the poetic practice of Sarah Kirsch. And it may be of value to consider examples of Sarah Kirsch's own artwork. Her six watercolours that adorn the volume of poems reissued to celebrate her sixtieth birthday in 1995, *Ich Crusoe*, offer, with all due allowance for the different demands of the mediums of paint and word, a remarkable commentary on her poetic practice: neither completely abstract nor representational, each picture suggests through its use of colour and shape the vigorous working of the poet's imagination, by turn clusters of shape explode or rise lightly and often unsystematically across the paper, the pastoral tones of some projecting a harmony that the shapes themselves do not inherently possess. No motif emerges strongly enough to suggest an all-embracing structure; the fascination resides in the individual elements, the background containing just the barest hint of harmony to prevent the total fragmentation of the activity in colour that these watercolours encapsulate. In her commentary to the pictures, 'Sarah Kirschs Ausflüge in die Aquarellmalerei', Karin von Maur aptly writes of an oscillation 'zwischen Tag und Traum'.[5] She adds:

> Das Erstaunliche dabei ist, daß Sarah Kirsch im Unterschied zu den meisten malenden Dichtern nicht das Motiv sucht, sondern sich ganz dem Medium der Wasserfarben und seinen spezifischen Ausdrucks-möglichkeiten anvertraut. Die schwerelose Zartheit ihrer Blätter resultiert aus der hingebenden Einfühlung in die Eigendynamik der Aquarellfarbe. So ergeben sich aus Fleckbildungen, Verlaufspuren oder Farbspritzern wie von sich motivische Anklänge, meist an Blüten oder Blätter, ohne jemals zu einer präzisen Gestaltform vorzustoßen.[6]

These comments can be transferred with a remarkable degree of appropriateness to Kirsch's work through the medium of language. Art has the advantage over both literature and music in that it displays all of itself simultaneously, the picture is revealed in its entirety at once, free from the constraints of a linear form, which dictates some ordering principle to marshal its material. It is precisely against these constraints that much of Kirsch's early poetry rubs in the poet's striving to be unfettered.

Just as Kirsch's poetic structures do not resolve themselves in clear pictures, so does her desire for individual freedom, in a poet who makes unashamed use of the first person, lead the reader to further unresolved elements in her early poetry. The wish to be free of constraints might suggest a stance ranging from the hedonistic to the apolitical, the purely aesthetic to the socially indifferent. Yet the early poems certainly do pick up social and political themes, and out of them some very bold assertions have been made on Kirsch's behalf, for both her early and later poetry.

Simply to remain working as a writer in East Germany was often interpreted as a political gesture, an act of identification. And in some of Sarah Kirsch's early volumes it is not difficult to find expressions that suggest a degree of commitment to the German Democratic Republic. The expressions of solidarity are never shrill, frequently preferring indirect and oblique references, sometimes working through the use of the negative, as, for example, in her initial and unflattering evocations of America.

The idea of East Germany as the 'better Germany' underlies the emotion, bitterly ironic in retrospect, that concludes her poem

'Fahrt II'. Here her country is, in the opening lines, evoked as a place, a state, offering protection and snugness: 'Aber am liebsten fahre ich Eisenbahn / durch mein kleines wärmendes Land' (*L*, 6). The poet is perfectly conscious of the divisions that have brought havoc to this land, and the name of Gryphius shows that Kirsch is working without codes, the talk is of Germany. The final stanza brings a rejection of the imagination to see any common ground with the other Germany:

> Die Fahrt wird schneller dem Rand meines Lands zu
> ich komme dem Meer entgegen den Bergen oder
> nur ritzendem Draht der durch Wald zieht, dahinter
> sprechen die Menschen wohl meine Sprache, kennen
> die Klagen des Gryphius wie ich
> haben die gleichen Bilder im Fernsehgerät
> doch die Worte
> die sie hörn die sie lesen, die gleichen Bilder
> werden den meinen entgegen sein, ich weiß und seh
> keinen Weg der meinen schnaufenden Zug
> durch den Draht führt
> ganz vorn die blaue Diesellok . . . (*L*, 7)

The text reinforces suggestions that the two Germanies are indeed growing apart, for there is implied doubt behind the use of 'wohl' in the line 'sprechen die Menschen wohl meine Sprache'. Nor does the poet shun the prospect of opposition and confrontation of ideologies between these two worlds, 'werden den meinen entgegen sein'. A year after the appearance of *Rückenwind*, however, Kirsch too was to take, figuratively speaking, the train to that other Germany when she moved to West Berlin in August 1977.

Her early verse contained not only expressions of loyalty and warmth towards that part of Germany in which she had begun to write; they also reveal affirmations of the ideology that that state represented. Kirsch chose not the path of direct exaltation, but one that was, doubtless, welcome to the state; in the following example from the poem 'Im Kreml noch Licht', the gentleness of Lenin's gesture towards the cat is offered as an image of his patient and tireless humanity, and by extension, the nobility of his political cause:

> Das ist Lenins weiße Katze
> Jede Nacht macht sie Patrouille

[. . .]
Führt ihr Weg zur Bibliothek
[. . .]
Und erinnert sich der Zeiten
Wie der eigenen Pfotenspuren
Als ihr Herr sie leise vermahnte
Und ein neues Blatt anfing. (Z, 27)

The reader must presume, or at least hope, that Kirsch was un-
aware of the same technique, to be found in Leni Riefenstahl's
Triumph des Willens, of linking the great leader with a gentle creature such as a cat.

Where Kirsch does directly enter the political arena in her early
poetry, it is with uneven success and little sense of new ground
being opened up. A Brechtian egalitarianism rings out from these
lines taken from the poem 'Sanssouci':

[. . .] König
es stünd dir besser an, du hättest dich
mit weniger Kleinen umgeben [. . .]
[. . .] wenn deine Gärten
auch sehr erlesen sind und die Schlößchen, obwohl
ich die eher zuschreib
den Gärtnern Steinmetzen Künstlern. (L, 52)

It is difficult to see what advance Kirsch has made here on the
sentiments expressed in Brecht's poem 'Fragen eines lesenden
Arbeiters'. Her response to the GDR as a progressive state,
improving the workers' lot, is generally composed in a minor key.
In the poem 'Petzow Kreis Werder', the former UFA studios,
which served the Nazi propaganda and entertainment machine
and produced such films as *Münchhausen*, have undergone trans-
formation: the Baron's 'zinniges Kitschschloß dient dem FDGB,
kleiner Fortschritt' (L, 39).

In general, however, Kirsch appears to be very much ill-at-ease
with the thought of being classed as a political poet and has
striven to rid herself of such a designation. What political verse
she has composed she has subsequently portrayed as an inevitable
product of her times and her context, and her following declar-
ation reads more as a concession than as an assertion of this
aspect of her poetic practice:

Ich habe Politik nie plakativ betrieben, aber natürlich sind in meine Texte ein bestimmtes Lebensgefühl und bestimmte Lebensumstände eingegangen, die mich als Einwohnerin der DDR kennzeichnen.[7]

Her poetry reveals that universal dilemma of the modern poet torn between the claims of the public and the private world in which even the slightest and most innocuous of gestures can no longer claim neutrality. The attempt to depoliticize the everyday and win for it the right of subjective mood was, by contrast, a particularly East German crisis. Guilt can lead to a state of paralysis, individuality can simply be wayward, as hinted at in the short text 'Schwarze Bohnen':

> Nachmittags nehme ich ein Buch in die Hand
> Nachmittags lege ich ein Buch aus der Hand
> Nachmittags fällt mir ein es gibt Krieg
> Nachmittags vergesse ich jedweden Krieg
> Nachmittags mahle ich Kaffee
> Nachmittags setze ich den zermahlenen Kaffee
> Rückwärts zusammen schöne
> Schwarze Bohnen
> Nachmittags ziehe ich mich aus mich an
> Erst schminke dann wasche ich mich
> Singe bin stumm. (Z, 9)

Kirsch's name has been associated not only with political verse in general: she has often been heralded in particular as a major champion of women. Her position amongst women writers has sometimes reached unprecedented and unrestrained adulation. One critical handbook devoted to European women writers has gone so far as to claim, 'Without a doubt, Sarah Kirsch is the most important German poet today',[8] whilst that fine observer of East German literature, Wolfgang Emmerich, stresses the theme of women's *Selbstbefreiung* as advocated by Kirsch's work. (Emmerich also offers an interesting reading of 'Schwarze Bohnen' as an unfulfilled love poem.)[9]

A closer look at the treatment of women in Kirsch's early poetry justifies a more cautious and qualified interpretation of the poet's position. In her early poetry unrequited or unsatisfactory love looms large in her choice of themes and inescapably creates a persistent image of unhappy women, but this is not reason enough to conclude that Kirsch is a champion or mouthpiece for

them. As in the case of her political stance Kirsch has found herself forced into a position of denying, or disassociating herself
from, the label of feminist writer: 'Ich bin nicht für irgendeine
politische Partei und werde mich keiner feministischen Bewegung
anschließen.'[10] This act of distancing herself finds expression in the
poem 'Männliches Steinbild im Park', the eleventh poem in her
Wiepersdorf cycle:

> Leider leider werden die Damen
> Immer schnurriger. Was die nicht mehr
> Können und alles vermögen! Die trenn sich
> Dreimal im Leben von Diesem und Jenem, die schleppen
> Nur das Nötige mit die Kinder, die Arbeit
> O wie mir graut! (*R*, 29)

Even if the reader allows for the fact that the picture of women is
distilled through a layer of irony, which rebounds against the
male perspective, it is still true to say that Kirsch's stance here is
more akin to one of sympathy or pity rather than of any overwhelming expression of identification with her sex. Kirsch's
poems betray too many expressions of the poet's own individuality to allow their sublimation into a wider statement on behalf of
her gender.

These early volumes in Sarah Kirsch's development mark a
struggle between private and social concerns; in this respect they
mirror the linguistic struggle between cohesion and energy that
they offer as texts. By the time that *Rückenwind*, the third of the
volumes considered here, had come to be written it was clear
which impulse had gained the upper hand in her work. The
result, however, had taken her outside the orbit of possibilities
offered by the German Democratic Republic. Even the plea for the
role of literature made by Stefan Heym at the end of the 1970s
held little relevance for her work:

> Literatur kann man nicht nach momentanen Gegebenheiten machen.
> Literatur muß auch in zwanzig oder fünfzig Jahren noch Gültiges über
> unsere Zeit aussagen. Wer das nicht sieht, wer die Kunst irgend-
> welchen taktischen Bedürfnissen unterwerfen will, vernichtet gerade
> die Kunst, die der Sozialismus braucht.[11]

Kirsch had through her poetry insisted on the right to be impul-
sive, to be politically aware or highly self-indulgent by turns, and

to utter ideas that coaxed readers who were willing to accept her markedly individual poetic form into sharing her conviction of poetry as an adventure and as movement, a gesture of personal liberation and an act of discovery: 'Ich lebe von der Entdeckung, von der Eroberung immer neuer Landschaften; ich erobere sie mir dann auch schreibend.'[12]

Notes

[1] *Grzimek's Animal Life Encyclopedia*, vol. 4, *Fishes I* (New York, Van Nostrand Reinhold, 1973), 363.

[2] Abbreviations used in this article refer to the editions listed on the abbreviations page apart from Z which refers to the 1974, Ebenhausen bei München, Langewiesche-Brandt edition.

[3] Gerd Labroisse and Ian Wallace (eds.), *DDR-Schriftsteller sprechen in der Zeit* (Amsterdam, Rodopi, 1991), 78.

[4] Marie Luise Kaschnitz, *Gedichte*, selected by Peter Huchel (Frankfurt am Main, Suhrkamp, 1975), 30.

[5] Sarah Kirsch, *Ich Crusoe: Sechzig Gedichte und sechs Aquarelle* (Stuttgart, Deutsche Verlags-Anstalt, 1995), 87.

[6] Ibid., 89.

[7] Labroisse and Wallace (eds.), *DDR-Schriftsteller*, 76

[8] Katharina M. Wilson (ed.), *An Encyclopedia of Continental Women Writers*, vol. 1, (London, St James Press, 1991), 637.

[9] Wolfgang Emmerich, *Kleine Literaturgeschichte der DDR* (Frankfurt am Main, Luchterhand, 1989), 224.

[10] Labroisse and Wallace (eds.), *DDR-Schriftsteller*, 76.

[11] Joachim Walther *et al.* (eds.), *Protokoll eines Tribunals. Die Ausschlüsse aus dem DDR-Schriftstellerverband 1979* (Reinbek bei Hamburg, Rowohlt, 1991), 47.

[12] Labroisse and Wallace (eds.), *DDR-Schriftsteller*, 75.

7

'Die Endlichkeit dieser Erde . . .':
Sarah Kirsch's Chronicles of Transience

MICHAEL BUTLER

Sarah Kirsch's status as a major figure in contemporary German poetry has long been acknowledged. Peter Hacks's well-known, if faintly mocking, appellation, the 'Sarah-Sound', merely underlines the unique quality of her poetic voice, its unmistakable rhythms and images. Paradoxically, however, Kirsch's principal work of the last decade has been devoted to prose rather than poetry: *Irrstern. Prosa* (1986), *Allerlei-Rauh. Eine Chronik* (1988), *Schwingrasen. Prosa* (1991), *Spreu* (1991) and *Das simple Leben* (1994). Only one major collection of poems, *Erlkönigs Tochter* (1992), interrupted this flow.[1] The reasons for this shift in emphasis are no doubt complex, but Sarah Kirsch herself has indicated that the concentration on prose was provoked by the realization that the form offered 'ein viel längeres Abenteuer noch als Gedichte'.[2] This in turn is clearly connected to a deeper interest in the possibilities of autobiographical writing, not in the conventionally subjective sense of relating the story of her life, but as a technical experiment in transmuting immediate personal experience into the discipline of objective form.

Naturally enough, with a writer of Sarah Kirsch's temperament, much of her prose work is akin to poetry, and even where she produces longer pieces, including narratives, her vocabulary and idiosyncratic syntax give these books the distinctively individual rhythms which readers will immediately recognize from her poetry. Indeed, *Drachensteigen* (1979), the collection which marked Kirsch's departure from the GDR and arrival in the FRG, had already placed prose and poetry side by side, thus indicating an equal fascination with both modes of expression.

What gives overriding unity to Kirsch's work, however, is not simply its linguistic tone, but above all the constancy of her themes. The ambiguities and paradoxes of her poetry, particularly the sense of a momentary idyll undermined by malign forces, all reappear in her prose. The possible exception to this persistent tone of melancholy transience is *La Pagerie* (1980), the brief account of a happy summer spent with a loved one in the eponymous chateau in the south of France. Clearly fuelled by an intoxicating mixture of freedom and energy after Kirsch's decision to leave the GDR in 1977, *La Pagerie* is an engagingly slight work, but one perhaps too swiftly dismissed as 'eine literarische Bagatelle'.[3] For though the sheer enjoyment of an exotic landscape with its sounds, vegetation and fragrances is the dominant inspiration of *La Pagerie*'s brief, impressionistic texts, there are – as always with Sarah Kirsch, if here not so obviously – darker moments amidst the superficial brilliance of a Provençal summer. For example, the famous tourist sites recall the religious intolerance of past centuries; the closed and neglected synagogue in Carpentras leaves the reader to flinch at the horror of more contemporary barbarism; after an imagined encounter with Petrarch and his lover Laura, the author's mind drifts to the remembered songs of young German soldiers in 1940 and their subsequent fate ('Wer weiß wie weiß die Knöchlein nun sind', *LP*, 54). Nor is Kirsch blind to the current problems of North African *Gastarbeiter* in the local vineyards, nor to the existential tragedy of her host's mentally ill young friend. Nevertheless, while the later prose works develop the techniques of *La Pagerie*, they never attempt to reproduce its basically optimistic tone and freedom of spirit. They thus remain more closely within the orbit of Kirsch's poetry.

The very title of *Irrstern* takes up the theme of transience which dominates most of Kirsch's work. Yet, paradoxically, these texts are firmly rooted in the flat, empty landscape of the Dithmarschen in south-western Schleswig-Holstein where the poet has lived since 1983. An older, more graphic word for a comet, 'Irrstern', suggests flashes of illumination which create the illusion of comprehending 'die Welt in einem Punkt' ('Mainacht', *I*, 22).[4] The book is characterized by a persistent tension between the desire to escape and the moral imperative of standing one's ground and accepting the burden of everyday commitments, including the duty of the poet to find expression for her perceptions. Thus the opening text, 'Hahnenschrei', sets the tone: the larks in the cold morning air contrast sharply with the motionless farmsteads anchored in mist 'wie vertäute Schiffe'; the farmers emerge for the day's toil whilst the narrator's inner eye gallops away over the dikes 'ohne an Umkehr zu denken'. With a beautiful modulation, Kirsch reins in such fantasy without destroying the breath of freedom it conveys: 'So aber wird man zu Fuß durch den löchrigen Nebel gehn seine Pflichten erfüllen' (*I*, 5).

Loosely structured on the seasons of a single year, *Irrstern* explores the ambiguity of shifting presences in this solid landscape. In 'Styx', for example, the River Eider, which nourishes the marshlands and their rich fauna, turns in a split second into the mythical river of the Underworld in which echo the 'Winseln und Schrein aller Wesen' (*I*, 42). Such dark fascination is only resisted by a swift return to mundanity where a single Yeatsian epiphany can transform the banal into something intensely magical:

> [. . .] es holt mir die Seele fast aus dem Leib wenn sich das Wunderbarste mit dem Gewöhnlichen verwischt und eine krummgebückte Alte hustend mit einem Hündchen den Deich heranschleicht. (*I*, 26)

In such an exactly observed environment – some twenty-seven species of birds are named! – the fragility of natural phenomena, including the ground itself, is powerfully conveyed. Only those with a delicate tread and an acute ear for Nature's intonation can escape for a moment the general sense of dislocation: 'Ein dumpfes Glück für den der es hört und noch auf der Sternenhaut geht federnd über die tiefen Moore' ('Vineta', *I*, 36). 'Doppelter Boden', indeed, is the title of one nightmarish vision in which the poet is hauled to account for her images by anonymous interrogators. The oblique reference to Karl-Marx-Stadt leaves the latter's identity in little doubt and reveals Sarah Kirsch's lasting contempt for the *Stasi*-regime she has left behind.

Thus the baleful shadow of politics is never far away even in this peaceful country retreat. Television, too, penetrates to every corner of the Dithmarschen, bringing insubstantial images, for example, of the Falklands conflict. Elsewhere, the noise of raucous starlings modulates into memories of childhood deprivation in the aftermath of war:

> Das Geräusch das die zusammenhaltenden Stare erzeugen ist ein Kinderwagenquietschen durch aufsitzende Türen, einhundert strapazierte Gefährte gleich nach 45 wenn eine ganze Straße ins Weichbild der Stadt aufbrach Kartoffeln und Kohlen wild zu erlangen. ('Starenwolken', *I*, 43)

Such events are frequently matched by a deeper, mythical level of uncertainty and loss. In 'Schwarzer Vogel'(*I*, 37), for example, Kirsch suddenly sees her own house with a stranger's eyes: 'Hier müssen glückliche Leute wohnen', she muses, yet only too well aware of the deceptive nature of appearances. Happiness is at best a fleeting experience – of mist, moor, animal, bird or plant – for we live inescapably in a post-Edenic world. Thus her garden is one of 'stürzender Bäume' where she has 'zwischen zwei Apfelbissen zuviel schon gewußt'. Defeating the arch-enemy *ennui* by changing landscapes, even countries, offers a merely temporary respite, but even then there is the fear that the country idyll is nothing more than theatrical scenery, 'unterirdisch durch Seile auf Rollen bewegt' (*I*, 37). This sense that her life – life itself – may be fundamentally counterfeit, 'einen streckenweise bekannten Film' (*I*, 38), sustains the melancholy tone that pervades even the brighter pieces in the collection. The 'Irrstern', she hints, is not a passing comet nor even Hölderlin's mythic sun, but the spinning earth itself: a land which offers no stability but boggy uncertainty: 'Der Sturm gibt die Richtung er kennt keinen Rückweg [. . .] Gräser dunkle Maulwurfshügel geneigtes abgestorbenes Holz begleiten uns lange' ('Stück Natur', *I*, 66).

If the often dreamlike quality of Kirsch's prose in *Irrstern* reveals the 'Schizophrenie unserer alltäglichen Existenz',[5] in *Allerlei-Rauh* she takes the technique an ambitious step forward. The book's subtitle, 'eine Chronik', points to her first attempt at a longer narrative structure in contrast to the laconic prose poems of *La Pagerie* and *Irrstern*. At the same time, the sense of an ongoing 'poetisches Logbuch' is particularly strong.[6] Indeed, the fundamental theme of this series of restrained autobiographical meditations on the nature of time is the fragility of memory and the fragmented nature of what Kirsch calls in her opening paragraph 'das Kaleidoskop unser Leben' (*A*, 7). The book's title, taken from the well-known tale in the Grimms' *Kinder- und Hausmärchen* suggests the technique of stitching disparate fragments – 'Rauhwerk allerlei Art' (*A*, 44) – to form a creative whole. In this case the varied 'pelts' are obtained from Kirsch's standard sources: daily routine and its minor tragedies, stories, dreams, memories of childhood, encounters with old friends in the GDR, together with meticulous observations of the fauna and flora of her Dithmarschen home.[7]

Despite the optimism inherent in the creative act of writing itself, the dominant tone of the book is one of mourning. But, as always with Sarah Kirsch, grief has both an intensely personal quality and a wider, historical, indeed existential dimension. Thus, on a return visit to the GDR her anger at the economic and ecological disintegration she observes takes her mind back to the Thirty Years' War and the resonant poetry of Andreas Gryphius in which the archetypal theme of transience is ironically expressed in the strict discipline of the sonnet form.[8] Such contemporary issues are balanced by the awareness of geological transitions: the discovery of fossils in the plains of Mecklenburg indicate the earlier domination of the sea and make Kirsch ponder on the consequences of global warming which may one day bring its return. The far from nostalgic memory of leaving the physical and mental isolation of a high-rise flat in East Berlin – 'ich hatte mich letzlich in meinem Hochhaus längst auf eine Hallig begeben, wo das ganze Jahr der Ruf Landunter! erscholl' (*A*, 89 f.) – leads to a moving passage on the death of a close friend. The bitter loss is only acceptable because it softens the fear of her own eventual demise: 'Wenn er schon tot ist, so kann ich leichter davon [. . .] Jetzt konnte ich in Staub zerfallen, wenn jemand wie er so eilig in Grund und Boden gerät' (*A*, 91). The rhythm of the sentences, the slightly archaic phrasing, capture exactly the sensibility of the *Barock* poets Kirsch so much admires.

The momentary flashes of happiness Kirsch experiences in the empty northern landscape are sustained, for all their brevity, by her trained biologist's eye for plants, animals and birds whose names, and therefore reality, are rapidly fading under the pressures of modern life. Images and metaphors flit past her readers as the products of 'das bunteste hilfreiche Kino im Kopf' (*A*, 36), inviting them to shape the evolving film with their own imagination.[9] But this is no 'Flucht zurück in die Natur',[10] but precisely its opposite: one hauntingly horrific image of a mole being eaten alive by maggots is enough to counter any form of neo-romanticism. Indeed, Sarah Kirsch expressly rejects 'die feige Flucht in die sanften Utopien' (*A*, 108). At the same time, the temptation to indulge in fashionable pessimism or complacent misanthropy in the face of the palpable 'Unheilbarkeit dieses Jahrhunderts' (*A*, 91) is firmly resisted. Despite the clear-sighted registration of human and natural destructiveness, the 'Chronik' ends not in morbidity, but on a strongly affirmative note. In a surprisingly Goethian turn of phrase Kirsch courageously embraces 'die Endlichkeit dieser

Erde': 'Ich bin dem Wechselhaften eingebunden, es scheint mir lange zu gehn' (*A*, 109).[11]

The ability to turn autobiographical material into prose of deeper resonance, already evinced in *Allerlei-Rauh*, is further demonstrated in Kirsch's next volume *Schwingrasen*, which returns to the formal qualities of the earlier texts, that is, denser, short pieces which stand on their own. But like *Allerlei-Rauh*, *Schwingrasen*, too, draws deeply on Kirsch's everyday occupations, particularly the problem of turning the unconsidered trifles of routine into art:

> Wie merkwürdig das ist: ich stand auf und da fast Vollmond herrschte konnte ich alles! draußen! vollständig sehen [. . .] Was vor vier Stunden wie Poesie sich doch ausnahm es ist stinkender Prosa gewichen. Eu Gott! Ich aber führe mein Journal hier getreulich. Am liebsten sehr früh in der Frühe, im Nichtmehr und Nochnicht. ('Das eine und das andere', *Sch*, 9)

The unstable moment between the past and the future is thus the most propitious time for locating the poetic quality of prosaic existence.

As befits the diary form, the tone of *Schwingrasen* is conversational; abbreviated spellings and slangy speech rhythms add to its colloquial flavour. At the same time, the book is not presented as a confessional *journal intime*:

> Ich will nicht mein Inneres abfotografieren weil ich mich nicht preisgeben will oder mich außerordentlich finde höchstens den Blickwinkel noch ein gewisses zärtliches Schielen aber das ist bloß das Lachen zwischen den Zeilen. ('Wie kommt Literatur zustande?', *Sch*, 34)

The sustained note of self-irony, and in particular the overt reflection on language and the culture industry at various points in the book, distinguish *Schwingrasen* from the earlier 'chronicle'. Thus between the more poetic texts Kirsch inserts a satire on the fashionable intellectual talk-show (her dismissive term is 'Talg-Show') which feeds on the vanity of writers.[12] For Kirsch, the task of artists is precisely to set their art against such 'Selbstherrlichkeit' ('Lachschleifen', *Sch*, 75). The self-publicizing performance risks the loss of all that matters, 'was Meister Gryphius den Seelenschatz nannte' (*Sch*, 76). Thus even the most private elements in this journal – painful recollections of the failure of her marriage to Rainer Kirsch – are presented in the semi-humorous, mythical guise of 'Prinz Herzlos'. The transience of human relationships can only be successfully controlled and expressed through the objective distance of self-irony.

The title of the collection – *Schwingrasen* is a meadow growing over marshland close to the sea – points to the basic uncertainty of the individual even when he or she has withdrawn from the destructive pressures of the city to the apparently safer ground of the countryside. Kirsch's descriptions of the hard life of the small farmers who must work this harsh land are devoid of pathos and so conjure up a unique mixture of defiant lyricism.[13] Kirsch's recurrent image of the 'Kino im Kopf' (*Sch*, 37) registers once again both pleasure in the peace of her isolated home in the village of Tielenhemme and awareness of the threat to its way of life posed, for example, by acid rain – a situation in which the poet can only project a warning voice into the void: 'Ich stecke seit Tagen im Leuchtturm fest und lasse das Nebelhorn schrein' ('Das Nebelhorn', *Sch*, 10). The theme of time, wisely spent or wasted, but always running out, is set by the brief three-sentence text, 'Zeitfresserin', which opens the collection. Whichever way one turns, the result is the same: 'Mein tapferes Herz schlägt wie eine Uhr und geht vorwärts und rückwärts kapores' (*Sch*, 7). The main point is that the writer retains her courage and her ability to articulate the beauty of what others wilfully ignore: 'Träumerisches Strandgut das Boot und die Kiste, in hohem Maß wertlos, unbrauchbar, schön' ('Strandgut', *Sch*, 42). Dreamily floating in her unique landscape, ninety per cent of which appears to be sky, she perceives stasis as the enemy: 'Mobilität is mein Segen gewesen' (*Sch*, 29). By this Kirsch means not simply escape from the personal and political constrictions of earlier existences, but more profoundly the crucial maintenance of a supple imagination.

In this context, the mass flight of GDR citizens over the Hungarian border which presaged the collapse of the communist regime takes on a more complex note – 'Da werden die Träume auch komplizierter' ('Wurzellos', *Sch*, 64) – for the collapse of rigid political systems warns of the vanity of distorted human aspirations, as does the most sombre text in the book, the concluding piece, 'Postludium'. With its trivializing eye, television sanitizes for home consumption the Gulf War and the Scud attacks on Israel, while 'geklonte Generäle' explain the finer points in ubiquitous studio discussions. Such horrors are subsumed in a single plangent sentence which recalls both Trakl and Celan: 'Ein schwarzer Regen ist mein Herz' (*Sch*, 85).

Published in the same year, *Spreu*, with its typically unpretentious title, records a series of reading tours undertaken at the behest of her publisher between May 1988 and December 1990, 'ne seltsame Art einen Lebensunterhalt zu verdienen', as she herself admits (*S*, 87). The diary which chronicles these 'Missionsreisen und Alphabetisierungsversuche' (*S*, 80) is prevented from degenerating into authorial arrogance by a pervasive but unobtrusive tone of self-mockery, underpinned by the casual, conversational tone familiar from its companion piece, *Schwingrasen*. What is different here is the physical presentation of the book, which at first sight resembles an attractive children's reader. Luxuriously printed, *Spreu* is copiously illustrated with prints from old zoology textbooks and encyclopaedias, coloured postcards, photomontage and pretty, abstract watercolours by the author herself. The fleeting images conjure up a tongue-in-cheek didacticism while at the same time creating a beautiful object as much as a literary text.[14]

However, the witty playfulness exhibited in *Spreu* – three mischievous 'corrigenda' point to 'errors' which do not exist, one indeed to page 218 in a book of 87 pages! – does not entirely sum up the book's compass. Although her diary principally annotates trips to southern Germany, Sweden and the Danish islands, Kirsch does touch, if only tangentially, on the political events of a particularly tumultuous moment in German history. A radio broadcast, 'Der Herbst 89 in der Literatur', caught late at night after a bizarre reading to a group of psychiatric patients, for example, elicits a cutting comment on former colleagues in the GDR and their pretentious illusions:

> Haben die Schriftsteller der DDR die Revolution vorbereitet? wird nun gefragt. Welche Revolution denn? [. . .] so viel Blindheit wie hier jeder Maulwurf besitzt. Die Autoren in der DDR würden meinen, sie stäken in einer Krise. Ach du schweiniges Vaterland du. Wie ist mein Zwerchfell erschüttert. Was es für ewige schlottrige Angsthasen doch sind. Verschlägt einem die Sprache' (*S*, 41).

More poignantly, she registers the continuing terrorist attacks on Jerusalem, placing in the margin of the page the Hebrew translation of her poem 'Wintermusik' by her Israeli friend, Asher Reich.

In one of the most resonant sentences in the book Kirsch sums up her response to the fragmentation of feeling such events symbolized as they are refracted through the media: 'Und nichts heileres auf der Welt als ein gebrochenes jüdisches Herz' (*S*, 81).

More than in any previous prose text, *Spreu* plays with language. Above all, visual humour is created not only by the incongruous illustrations, but also by curious spellings, often phonetic renderings of dialect or regional accent (for example, 'Göld', 'Artikul', 'Insul', 'Interwjuh', 'Akwareller', 'Bißchen wat Dekoratiefes', 'Steuerbescheud', 'Konsthall', 'ich loch mich kronk') and deliberate archaisms (for example, 'itzt', 'diesz', 'viereley musses wohl seyn', 'viel Geschrey'). These mild linguistic jokes may well be a nod of affection to Ernst Jandl and the experimental work of the *Wiener Gruppe* – H. C. Artmann makes a brief appearance (*S*, 71) – but there is a strained air about some of these coinings which suggests that Kirsch is growing uncertain about how to handle her material. Nevertheless, *Spreu* is certainly the least complicated of her texts since *La Pagerie*. And the danger that critics might seek for profundities which are not in fact there is a phenomenon that Sarah Kirsch herself – somewhat defensively? – points out: 'Was die alles rausgekriegt haben aus meinen bescheidenen Texten man darf sich bloß wundern' (*S*, 73).

However modest the intentions behind *Spreu* may or may not have been, Kirsch's latest volume of prose, *Das simple Leben*, returns the reader to familiar ground. Indeed, *Erlkönigs Tochter*, her first collection of poems since *Schneewärme* (1989), had already re-established her more customary sombre tone. These poems are dominated by the inhospitable cold of winter landscapes which occasionally produce a despairing nostalgia as in 'Ferne':

> Niemals wird auf den
> Armen Gefilden Herrlichkeit
> Liegen wie in der Kindheit als noch die
> Fichten grün und licht lebten.
> Schwarzes
> Wissen beugt mir den Hals (*ET*, 65)

Associated with the loss of childlike spontaneity is the fear that her writing has become 'ein Strom von Wiederholungen'. In a bleak reply to Rilke's notion of aesthetic celebration, the poem 'Der Chronist', continues:

[. . .] Und Grauen
Entspringt der zitternden Hand. Sie wandert

Bei Tag und bei Nacht elend übers Papier.
Zu preisen gibt es heut nicht mehr viel.

Und deshalb ist des Schreibens müde die Hand. (*ET*, 61)

Such a bleakly defeatist note is rare in Sarah Kirsch's poetry which has hitherto navigated the paradox of how to articulate losses of articulacy with considerable skill. *Das simple Leben*, however, only partially succeeds in defeating such black moods. In her own words, this detailed chronicle of a single year, 1991, is one more instalment 'in meinem Roman den ich in solche Hefte hier schreibe. Ein langes Werk' (*SL*, 31). The problem is that much of the book gives off an air of *déjà vu*, intensified by the old tricks of unconventional spellings and syntax which are themselves in danger of degenerating into cliché. Indeed, in a faintly incestuous way, the diary accompanies and comments on the composition of *Schwingrasen*, *Spreu*, and *Erlkönigs Tochter* to the extent of frequent quotation. Yet *Das simple Leben* is not a tour of the writer's workshop. Although Kirsch sighs that her book is 'neu und ohne Charakter' (*SL*, 5), it soon takes on familiar contours. For example, horror at public events – the revelations of ever more *Stasi* scandals in the GDR, the Gulf War and the nascent tragedy in the Balkans, TV programmes on Dachau and the Chernobyl disaster, German unity celebrations and the attacks on asylum-seekers – is countered by the attempt to create private order in her garden in Tielenhemme. However, this response does not announce a belated flight from reality, a final retreat behind the dikes of the Dithmarschen. On the contrary, as in all her work, Kirsch continues to hold the conflicting tensions between the impersonal juggernaut of history, despair at human depredation and love for the transient beauty of the natural environment, even though her rage occasionally peters out into impotent irony: 'Es fällt mich in solchem Moment eine unglaubliche Wut auf die parasitären Menscher und die Zustände des Planeten glatt an und so weiter' (*SL*, 23 f.). A visit to Greifswald, too, fuels unproductive anger at the ecological devastation and the decay of whole villages, as she rails at the meek acquiescence of the East Germans who put up with this dismal reality for so long.

As with her previous prose texts, *Das simple Leben* is full of teasing ambiguities, not least suggested by the adjectival foreign word in the book's title: the book demonstrates that beneath the trivial surface there is nothing in fact simple about 'das simple Leben'. Even in the relatively unspoilt countryside of Schleswig-Holstein, things are rarely what they seem, and there can be no guarantee of permanence in the happiness momentarily gained from intimacy with partner, child and friends or with animals, flora and fauna. The weakness of the book, however, lies in its self-referentiality. Kirsch has always based her prose texts on the minutiae of her everyday life, but here autobiographical matters often come too close to an obsessive self-centredness. The reader who is not privy to the trials and tribulations of her friends, identified only by their Christian names, grows quickly irritated, and interest in their doings evaporates. On the other hand, there can only be admiration for the steadfastness of Kirsch's dedication to her craft. More than in any previous volume of this kind, the reader can appreciate Kirsch's affinity with the *Barock* tradition. The solemn music for 'Totensonntag', for example, appeals to her acute sense of the transience of all things: 'Ich habe sowieso gern was vom Tod um die Ohren' (*SL*, 30). But against this morbid fascination with what on another occasion she calls the 'Zeitfresser' (*SL*, 26) is set a clear and positive statement: 'Jeder Augenblick ist absolut' (*SL*, 25). This assertion that the poet's task is to grasp and identify the unique value of each moment in the anonymous flux of time provides the key to the sustained vitality of Kirsch's work.

Nevertheless, *Das simple Leben* appears to have taken the 'chronicle' form to its limits. Joachim Kaiser, in a perceptive review, acknowledged the attractiveness of Kirsch's prose when he described its essence as 'skurrile Verzweiflung, verzweifelte Skurrilität'.[15] Indeed, linguistic wit and a fine sense of the comic in human affairs have always attenuated or controlled the darker side of Sarah Kirsch's preoccupations. At the same time, her ability to give fresh expression to the final earthiness of things, 'die Endlichkeit dieser Erde', to perceive solidity amidst the impermanence that continually threatens to engulf her, gives the kaleidoscopic images that crowd her personal 'Kino im Kopf' their distinctive tone and form.

Notes

[1] Abbreviations used in this article refer to those on the abbreviations page apart from *LP* which refers to *La Pagerie* (Munich, Deutscher Taschenbuch Verlag, 1986).

[2] Quoted in Heide Soltau, 'Kleiner Ort mit großem Himmel', *Deutsches Allgemeines Sonntagsblatt*, 11 May 1986.

[3] Jürgen P. Wallmann, 'Arme Landschaft, reiche Sprache', *Der Tagesspiegel*, 24 August 1986.

[4] Hölderlin uses the word for the sun ('Irrstern des Tages') in his ode 'Chiron', the theme of which is the resolution of existential dissonance.

[5] Heinz Ludwig Arnold, 'Traumprosa', *Frankfurter Rundschau*, 29 July 1986.

[6] Harald Hartung coined the term in his review of *Irrstern*: 'Die Doppellast der Dichterin', *Frankfurter Allgemeine Zeitung*, 3 May 1986.

[7] Kirsch includes a reworking of the original *Märchen* with a modern ending (the saviour-king becomes a post-war GI, and the couple live happily ever after in Wiesbaden!). The point of this playful adaptation of the archetypal theme of a high-born female's social degradation preceding secular redemption is obscure. However, the notion of truth eventually shining through a deceptively crude exterior could be taken as a metaphor for Kirsch's poetic method in general. 'Allerleih-Rauh' is also the title of the first section of *Drachensteigen* and of a poem within it.

[8] Cf. Kirsch's reply to Gunna Wendt on what she grieves for in the former GDR: 'kaputtgemachte Städte. Entsetzlich zugrundegegangene Landschaften [. . .]. Wenn ich an Städte denke wie Stralsund, das dreht mir das Herz um. Manches hat den Dreißigjährigen Krieg und sonstwas überlebt, aber nicht vierzig Jahre DDR. Das ist etwas ganz Schmerzliches, auch was Natur betrifft', in 'Man muß nicht immer in der Hauptstadt sein. Ein Gespräch mit Sarah Kirsch', *Frankfurter Rundschau*, No. 89, Easter 1995. See also Peter Graves, 'Sarah Kirsch: Some comments and a conversation', *German Life and Letters*, 44 (1991), 271–80, here 275.

[9] Cf. Kirsch's remark to Wendt; 'Das Kino im Kopf ist ja tausendmal besser als das, was es im Fernsehen gibt. Aber man muß dann selber denken, und das verlernen die Leute leider ein bißchen.' (See note 8).

[10] Peter Molu, 'Zurück zur Natur – eine Flucht? Sarah Kirschs autobiographische Chronik', *Die Presse*, 23–24 April 1988. Karl Riha is closer to the mark when he notes traces of a currently fashionable 'Neoromantik' but concludes: 'Was zählt, ist eine vom Erschrecken geprägte Imagination, die den Leser wirklich in die Tiefe reißt', in 'Neoromantik. Sarah Kirschs bukolisches Prosabuch *Allerlei-Rauh*', *Frankfurter Rundschau*, 9 April 1988.

[11] Cf. Goethe's poem, 'Dauer im Wechsel'.

[12] An example of such 'Talg-Shows' – though in this case reserved mainly for self-important critics – would be Marcel Reich-Ranicki's popular TV programme, *Das literarische Quartett*, in which the parading of egos is all too often in reverse proportion to the light thrown on the books discussed.

[13] Joachim Kaiser characterizes Kirsch's writing as 'trotzig und lyrisch zugleich', in 'Heiter bockige Einsiedlerin', *Süddeutsche Zeitung*, 16–17 November 1991.

[14] With some justification Peter von Matt dubbed *Spreu* 'ein Buch für Anhänger, eine Jahresausgabe für den S.K.-Fan-Club', in 'Schwingrasen und Spreu. Die Prosa der Dichterin Sarah Kirsch', *Frankfurter Allgemeine Zeitung*, 8 October 1991. Indeed, the success of *Spreu* was immediate: a second edition was required a mere eight weeks after the first.

[15] 'Kleines Meisterwerk und größere Hoffnung', *Süddeutsche Zeitung*, 17 March 1994.

8

'Es riecht nach Tang, Salz und Wahrheit': Sarah Kirsch in Wales

MERERID HOPWOOD

Sarah Kirsch has visited Wales twice, both times as the guest of the German Department at University of Wales Swansea. She recorded the impressions of her first stay in three poems published in the volume *Erlkönigs Tochter*, namely 'Mumbles Bay' (*ET*, 38–9), 'Stechginster' (*ET*, 40) and 'Brief' (*ET*, 41). Her second stay gave rise to a short film for the Westdeutsche Rundfunk, the title of which I have borrowed for this article and which first appeared as the opening line for another poem in *Erlkönigs Tochter*, 'Springflut' (*ET*, 11).[1] It was as a result of this second stay that she also wrote the five poems published for the first time in this volume.

The aim of this article is twofold. Firstly I should like to place the Welsh poems in the context of Kirsch's work as a whole, showing how some of the themes and images which dominate these latest compositions have characterized her writing over three decades. Secondly I should also like to comment on the poems as a Welsh reader and as someone who helped Sarah Kirsch make the Welsh connection, though I must stress that it is certainly not my aim to close the 'open spaces' inherent in the poems with any pretence at authority which may be falsely based on a privileged 'biographical' approach of this kind. Kirsch attaches much importance to allowing the reader 'einen Spielraum',[2] and I believe with Wolfgang Iser that it is precisely the spaces in literary texts which present the reader with the interpretative challenge which makes reading them both enjoyable and purposeful.[3] In the interview in Chapter Three of this book Kirsch answers the suggestion that references to specific and often unknown people and places in her texts can baffle the reader with the words: 'Auch ein Rätsel kann schön sein', and so my comments on the circumstances which inspired the Welsh poems are offered as clues

rather than solutions and will, I hope, add a further dimension to
them.

Sarah Kirsch first came to Swansea in 1989. The city was at that
time familiar to her only as the birthplace of one of its famous
sons, Dylan Thomas (1914–53), and it is not difficult to recognize
his influence on the style of 'Mumbles Bay' and 'Stechginster' in
particular, where, at times, one feels that it is perhaps parodied
rather than imitated and where, as I will show later, some of his
well-known images are simply and unashamedly translated.

Mumbles is the gateway to the beautiful Gower coastline, three
miles or so west of the university campus along Swansea Bay. The
poem 'Mumbles Bay' describes one evening which Sarah Kirsch
spent exploring the coastal village, with the sea and its fishing
boats on the one hand and its many pubs on the other. It is set
against the background of a dark and stormy evening, but in spite
of the weather it is on the whole a carefree poem; as such, it is
uncharacteristic of Kirsch's work as a whole, for she gives expression more often to darker emotions such as fear and sadness.[4] By
contrast, a light-hearted, almost nonsensical tone is created in the
opening stanza of 'Mumbles Bay':

> Weil und obgleich es ne sehr finstere
> Nacht ist – sternlos und bibelschwarz wie es
> Heißt – sehe ich mich am Rand der Keltischen
> See und mein grauäugiger Gastgeber sagt
> Daß unsere Vorgänger (deutschsprachiger
> Vortragsreisender dienstältester Germanistik-
> Professor) ihrerzeit hier im klapprigen
> AUSTIN sitzenblieben bei Nebel und
> Wahnsinnsregen den weißen Mittelstreifen
> Nicht zu verlieren. So hatte wohl jeder
> Sein eigenes Meer oder der Schweizer keins. (*ET*, 38)

Both Kirsch's visit to Mumbles with Professor Rhys W. Williams
(her 'grauäugiger Gastgeber') and her reworking of the experience
in literary form have their antecedents. Professor Morgan
Waidson, Professor Williams's predecessor as the 'dienstältester
Germanistik- / Professor' in Swansea, had taken the Swiss writer
Jürg Amann to see the sights of Mumbles in similarly inclement
weather. Amann turned the bizarre experience into the short prose
piece 'Marbles-Bay':

Ein junger Vortragsreisender, der zum erstenmal im Leben nach dem walisischen Swansea kam, wurde vom dienstältesten Professor der dortigen Universität vom Bahnhof abgeholt. Es goß in Strömen. Dichter Nebel hatte selbst auf dem Bahnsteig das Erkennen nur nach der Beschreibung schwer gemacht. Trotzdem hielt der Eingesessene an seiner Absicht fest, seinen Gast zu der Sehenswürdigkeit des Küstenstrichs zu bringen. In seinem alten Austin fuhren sie ins Graue hinein. Einziger Halt für das Auge war die weiße Mittellinie der gewundenen Straße. Links wäre das Meer, sagte der Professor.

Der Wagen rollte auf ein Parkfeld hinaus, auf einen Randstein zu, blieb stehen. Der Professor beugte sich vor, wischte mit den Händen die Scheibe klar. Die Marbles-Bay, sagte er. Der Wind warf den Regen gegen das Glas. Der Motor war abgestellt, nur der Scheibenwischer schwamm hin und her. Sie starrten auf den Kühler, der vor ihnen in den Nebel hinaus ragte. Ich sollte vielleicht etwas sagen, dachte der Fremde. Aber er sagte nichts. Endlich warf der Professor den Motor wieder an, legte den Rückwärtsgang ein, fuhr an. Man sieht nichts, sagte er. Man sieht nichts, sagte sein Gast.[5]

Kirsch's direct allusions to Amann's text are obvious from the above. Just as she and Professor Williams follow in the footsteps of Amann and Professor Waidson, so, in writing about the previous visit, she turns her own poem into a successor to Amann's description. In Kirsch's 'Mumbles Bay' the colloquial use of 'wahnsinn' as an adverb is used to great effect as the phrase 'es regnet *wahnsinnig viel*' is turned into a compound noun, 'Wahnsinnsregen', to evoke a topsy-turvy world in which the two men in Amann's account endeavour to hold on to their sanity by keeping sight not of the proverbial 'roter Faden' of a discussion but of the white line in the middle of the road ('weisser Mittelstreifen'). Any reverence towards her predecessors which may have been suggested by this intellectual effort and by the adjective 'dienstältester' is shown to be meant ironically as she reiterates the curiously comic situation in which her Swiss counterpart found himself: trapped in an old 'banger' of an Austin car in the pouring rain, trying to enjoy the Mumbles coastline.

A pause at the end of the first stanza is not long enough to ponder on any deep significance which may be hinted at in the sentence 'So hatte wohl jeder / Sein eigenes Meer [. . .]', as it is quickly shrugged off with the quirky rejoinder 'oder der Schweizer keins'. The apparent lack of coherence between the two sentences, despite the fact that they are joined by 'oder', continues

into the second stanza where a drunken atmosphere is evoked as
the word 'jedenfalls' in the first line bears no obvious relation to
anything which precedes it. The 'I' of the poem boasts (as drunks
often do) that it, in contrast to the earlier visitors to the village,
can easily make out the sea and the pub and the fishing boats,
and that the visit to that first pub was only just the beginning!
The humorous exaggeration grows, with the number of pubs
visited set at seventeen and as the stanza progresses the effect of
the beer is anticipated as the scenery is perceived through the
senses of sight, smell and sound, and intoxicates the mind: 'Das
ging mir / [. . .] strikt in den Kopf'. Later, in the third stanza,
the use of alliteration: 'Der Sturm / Riss Trichter und Treppen
eisige Schneisen', seems to imitate the slurring speech of
drunkenness and in the same tone the poetic voice repeats itself as
the pub and the beer are both compared with paradise: 'Garten
Eden' (line 22) and 'außerirdisch' (line 26). The pub is offered as a
sanctuary from the storm outside with the comfort of its typical
plush-velvet upholstered chairs. Although these are set alongside
the less welcoming and less typical sword fish (which actually
hangs in The Pilot tavern in Mumbles), the addition of the dim-
inutive *-chen* to both the sword fish and furniture ensures that the
former loses any frightening aspect it may have, and is another
expression of the bizarre paradoxes which characterize 'Mumbles
Bay'.

The poem is full of local colour and here again as in a number
of her poems – e.g. 'Stiefmütterchen' (*I*, 20),[6] 'Two Magpies' (*ET*,
43),[7] 'Mauer' (*ET*, 7),[8] and 'Angeln mit Sascha' (*Z*, 32)[9] – Kirsch
shows that she has no reservations about referring quite specifically to the events, people and places which brought the poems
into existence. The use of capital letters to highlight proper nouns,
however, is unique to this poem and is a device which further
enhances the authenticity of the poem's location: 'AUSTIN',
'PILOTEN', 'KING ARTHUR', and to the same effect, indirect
speech is recorded through the (somewhat uncertain) usage of the
English phrases 'a quarter', 'a pint', and 'lady'.

In the penultimate sentence of the poem the reader catches a
glimpse of a more familiar Sarah Kirsch as she voices concern
about the state of her soul, 'Der Seele Kernhaus', which is turned
inside out by the storm and made to rattle in the wind. Yet, even
here, a light-hearted tone is quickly retrieved as the poem closes
with the picture of sheep queuing up to wait for a bus, which is

more of a tongue-in-cheek comment on the British custom of queue-forming than any philosophical observation! It does remind one of Kirsch's fascination with sheep, however, revealed perhaps most clearly in the prose collection *Irrstern*, in particular in 'Schäferstündchen' (*I*, 33) , 'Sonne und Mond' (*I*, 15), 'Styx' (*I*, 41), 'Wettersturz' (*I*, 13), and 'Auf dem Deich' (*I*, 17) where sheep are said to be 'die sehr klugen Tiere', or 'Vorwort' (*I*, 10), which begins with the sentence: 'Es gelüstet mich seit langem einen Text über Schafe zu schreiben etwas Endgültiges aus ihrem Leben berichten'. Even though listing adjectives one after the other and creating new adjectives out of nouns has been the hallmark of Kirsch's poetry since her very early publications, in the context of Swansea it is difficult not to hear the influence of Dylan Thomas on this aspect of her style, especially as one's ears are opened to the echoes of Thomas in the direct translations from *Under Milk Wood*: 'sternlos', 'bibelschwarz', 'klingenden Flaschen', which in typical Thomas style create rushed snapshot images where nouns are used as adjectives and verbs. Even the name of the boat which the poet is able to make out in the bay – 'STERN VON WALES' – is a translation of the 'Star of Wales' which appears in *Under Milk Wood*; one is reminded of the fact that, as a student in the GDR, Kirsch swapped her copy of a first-edition volume of poems by Gottfried Benn for a copy of Thomas's text.[10]

The Gower coastline in May is covered with the gorse bush in bloom, a prickly wild shrub with a deep yellow flower. It is also the lambing season, and it is these images that 'Stechginster' evokes as it begins with its description of the sea and landscape of Swansea. The first line is taken from Dylan Thomas's 'Fern Hill',[11] and it is worth noting that a translation of 'Fern Hill' appears in the first section of Enzensberger's influential *Museum der modernen Poesie* – an anthology which Kirsch admits had a great influence on her as a young poet in the GDR.[12] The sixth and final stanza of Thomas's 'Fern Hill' begins: 'Nothing I cared, in the lamb white days', the second clause of which is paraphrased by Kirsch in the opening line of 'Stechginster': 'Es begannen die lammweißen Tage'. But this is not the only point of similarity between 'Fern Hill' and 'Stechginster'. The poets' palettes of colours in both poems consist mainly of white, green and gold. White is evoked in expressions such as: 'lammweißen Tage', 'neuerstandene Wolken', 'Lämmer' in the Kirsch poem, and in the Thomas poem in references such as these: 'daisies', 'lamb white days', 'the moon', 'the farm like a wanderer white'. Green is used by Kirsch to describe the farmhouses: 'Bauernhöfe Grün bis unter die Tür', and by Thomas in phrases such as 'apple bough', and 'long as the grass was green'. Gold is evoked in the Kirsch poem in her references to 'Stechginster', 'Ginsterblüte', 'Dunkelgelb die Lichter' and 'Sand', and in the Thomas poem in the phrases 'Golden in the heyday of his eyes' and 'Before the children green and golden'. In making these comparisons, however, one should point out that, while it may be a self-conscious decision on Kirsch's part to copy the colour scheme here, it is not the first time that she has been attracted to these colours in the surrounding countryside. The first sentence of 'Spielraum' (*I*, 29), for example, reflects all three colours: 'Die unermüdliche Sonne und Lämmerwolken erschaffen ein Schachbrett auf grünendem Land'. Similarly, while one can see further parallels between 'Fern Hill' and 'Stechginster' in the reference to the farmhouse and clouds in the first stanza, to the sheep in the second and to the owl and the wild horses in the third, it must be said that here, too, it is possible to trace in earlier compositions by Kirsch abundant instances which make use of the very same elements, as in 'Käuzchen' in 'Lachen' (*R*, 68) or 'Die Welt ist ein Gehöft im Winter' in 'Eichen und Rosen' (*K*, 6). The similarity between the first part of the last sentence of the Kirsch poem and the last four lines of the third stanza in the Thomas poem, however, is unmistakable and must be more than coincidental.[13] Kirsch uses the images of 'Fern Hill' and rearranges them to create, through their new constellation, a new poem.[14] Compare:

> [. . .] Das donnernde Meer
> Das Traben wilder Pferde im Traum
> Als die Käuze jagten [. . .]

with:

> As I rode to sleep the owls were bearing the farm away,
> All the moon long I heard, blessed among stables, the nightjars
> Flying with the ricks, and the horses
> Flashing into the dark.

If the author of 'Fern Hill' is caught out by the innocence of youth only to realize at a more mature age that in the past he had

been a carefree prisoner of time: 'Time held me green and dying /
Though I sang in my chains like the sea', the poet of 'Stechginster'
is much more aware of the darker side of life and is much less
naïve. Like the voice in 'Dritter Monat' (Z, 61) which was
reminded by the robin 'Daß aus Beeren Blüten werden', the poetic
voice in 'Stechginster' knows from the start that the beautiful
golden gorse bush hides under its flowers a prickly thorn (that the
title should be 'Stechginster' and not the gentler synonym –
'Ginsterblüte' – suggests that this darker side is foremost in the
poet's thoughts), and she knows too that the sea has both a high
and low tide. The poet is defenceless against the elements of
nature as the 'änglischen Schuhe' keep the water in rather than
out, and the 'I' of the poem is left to squelch along the beach with
a pack of barking dogs. While the ships are said to 'glide' past on
what one would assume must therefore be calm waters 'vorüber /
Gleitender Schiffe', the sea is said to thunder on: 'Das donnernde
Meer', and the suggestion that the storm described here is an
inner, emotional storm is strengthened as the poem continues to
compare the thundering of the sea with the galloping of wild
horses in a dream. The dark yellow, man-made street-lights of
Swansea (typical of Britain, but not of Germany where the streets
are usually lit with white lights) confuse the poet and become the
stars or the gorse flowers which can only be seen in the inverted
reflection of a mirror. Here it is difficult for anybody familiar with
Kirsch's work not to be reminded of other instances where a mirror is used to suggest loneliness and deceit, in particular the piece
in *La Pagerie* (*LP*, 56) that ends 'Ein Spiegel mit mir darin, weil
sonst niemand da ist'.

The significance of the reference to birds and of the imagery of
flying in general, as well as the role of water in this poem, will be
treated later in the course of the discussion on the five poems of
Kirsch's second visit, but I cannot leave 'Stechginster' without
drawing the reader's attention to a particular feature of its pros-
ody. During Kirsch's stay in Wales she was introduced to the
ancient Welsh tradition of writing poems in *cynghanedd*. According
to the strict *cynghanedd* rules, which are at least twelve hundred
years old and probably much older,[15] a line of poetry must contain
elements of internal rhyme, whether it is consonantal or vowelled
or both. There are four basic types of *cynghanedd*: *Croes* (consonantal), *Traws* (partly consonantal), *Sain* (both vowelled and consonantal) and *Llusg* (vowelled), and it is interesting to note that at

least three lines in 'Stechginster' (8, 11 and 15) and arguably two
more (2 and 6) contain elements of the *cynghanedd*. The diagram
below shows the *cynghanedd* elements of lines 8, 11 and 15:

```
Mit einer  Meute klaffender   Hunde
M t    (er) M   t          nd(er)    nd
Reisten auf der  Reling vorüber
R           (er)  R         r  (er)
Das Traben wilder Pferde im Traum
    Tr        er    er       Tr
```

To what extent Dylan Thomas himself made conscious use of the
cynghanedd in his work has been a much debated question and I
can do no better than to refer the reader to Alan Llwyd's essay in
Poetry Wales[16] for an introduction to this matter and an overview
of how *cynghanedd* has been used by other non-Welsh-speaking
writers outside Wales during the twentieth century, and to Donald
Evans's essay in the same volume for a general study of the rudi-
ments of the *cynganeddion*. Whatever the eventual outcome of that
debate, the strong alliteration of Kirsch's Welsh poem does at least
suggest some influence of the *cynghanedd*.

   In 'Brief', a short poem of six lines, the reader is offered an
orientation of Swansea. Dispensing with the compass, Kirsch, as
she lies in bed, situates the town between the sea at her feet and
the hills behind her. Distance is shown to be a relative concept as
the casual 'geradeaus' is used to locate far-away America as if it
were a suburb of the Mumbles. In the same local, almost naïve,
register the market-place is mentioned. However, the market-place
becomes not the usual harmless centre of trade in a typical town
but rather a sinister landmark which bears the scarring of the German bombing raids on Swansea during the Second World War.
And the reference to this unhappy past relationship between
Wales and Germany shatters the present idyll. Through rhyme the
pair of words: 'Füßen' and 'Rücken' are linked to the three words
'Lücken', 'unseren' and 'Bomben', but despite their soothing 'en'
sound and lulling rhythm the dramatic contrast in content reveals
Sarah Kirsch's preoccupation with the dark aspect she finds
almost always lurking behind any apparently innocent setting.[17] In
this way the mood of the poem is totally transformed over six
short lines from contentment in the first line, 'Es ist schön jetzt', to
the uneasy image of the devastation of war. The banal adverb

'schön' is used here to the same effect as the adjective 'nett' in the first prose piece in *Irrstern* (*I*, 5), 'Es ist ein nettes Gefühl', where an initially harmless tone creates a false sense of security as the texts develop to describe scenes which are far less idyllic.

Five years later Sarah Kirsch returned to Wales. The landscape is the same but the tone and themes of the poems are changed. The dark moods felt occasionally in 'Mumbles Bay', 'Stechginster' and 'Brief' now dominate the desperate and hopeless cadences of her work and in the return to the theme of unrequited love the reader hears the echo of the voice from some of the *Zaubersprüche* poems – 'Ich wollte meinen König töten' (*Z*, 10) and 'Märchen im Schrank' (*Z*, 14) for example.[18] However, this time there is more anguish and less resilience. In this second sequence of the Welsh poems there is no dream of revenge but an overwhelming sense of hopelessness and resignation as the offended lover seems to accept that relationships between lovers are destined for unhappy endings. In 'Gwyll', 'Caswell Bay', 'Auflaufendes Wasser Vollmond' and 'Seestück' the 'I' of the poem either watches or waits for the object of its love from a distance and is unable to close the gap between them. In 'In den Wellen', too, there is a sense of longing, and again it is not clear whether the first person will ever join the second person in a brighter, summery, future. During her second stay Kirsch composed at least another three poems which sadly she has since withdrawn from the collection, and while her wishes not to have them published must of course be respected, it is fair to say that these were similar in tone. Each of the poems draws heavily on the Gower countryside and coastline for its imagery, and in another poem, 'Spottdrossel' (first recited by Kirsch in the *Entdeckungen* film and written during her second stay in Wales),[19] Nature becomes the accomplice not of the lyrical 'I' but of the other, as a mockingbird refuses to reveal the secrets of the other's heart and leaves the 'I' of the poem derided and alone.

Caswell Bay is a cove about a quarter of a mile from the house in which Kirsch stayed in May 1994. The final version of the poem which bears its name is in no way altered from the first draft, which suggests that Kirsch composed it spontaneously and in its final form. It was one of only two poems of the original collection that she was happy to include for publication in this volume ('Gwyll' was the other). It begins with a description of two static creatures, the limpet and the starfish, awaiting their destiny in the shape of the tide which will release them from captivity. Alone they cannot escape from the prison of their dark caves – their fate depends on the sea.

After this opening sentence the poem continues to describe the relationship between the first and second person. The second person is a free spirit, changed and changing like the smoke of a pipe or cigarette. It has the ability to rise above the cliffs. It is vaporous and thus cannot be caught. The first person by contrast is the shadow of the second person and so depends on the second for its very existence. Through the image of the shadow, the relationship between them is portrayed in a highly romanticized way, for whilst they are inseparable, the bond between them remains intangible. The idiosyncratic use of the archaic form 'Schatte' (seen in other poems by Kirsch such as 'Elegie I' (Z, 18), 'Ich bin ein Schatte geworden im Sommer') contributes to the romanticization of the scene,[20] as does the detail of the blue hyacinth behind the ear. The shadow as an inadequate substitute either for the poet or for others is often used by Kirsch, as for example in 'Immer' (R, 72) where the first and second persons as in 'Caswell Bay' are joined only through shadows: '[. . .] oft / Unter die Füße mein Schatten / Mischt sich in deinen'. There are further examples in 'Unterwegs' (Lw, 155) and in the eighth poem of 'Reisezehrung' (E, 44) where the shadows are memories which will never disappear.[21]

The images of the second part of the poem (lines 2–6) add further dimensions to its possible meaning. The limpet is a mollusc with a soft body protected by a hard outer shell. When the tide is out it clings tightly to the rock making it virtually impossible to dislodge. When the tide returns it is able to move in order to feed on seaweed before it settles back to exactly the same spot on the rock where it has worn away a tiny hollow home for itself. The starfish on the other hand feeds on molluscs. It pulls steadily on them for a long time in order to release them, and then devours them by pushing its stomach through its mouth and wrapping it around them, until at last they have been digested. Since the starfish consumes molluscs such as the limpet, it could be said that it is more powerful than the limpet. Yet without the movement and force of the tide, it too is stranded, and though it is a threat to the limpet's existence, it needs that existence in order to survive.

In view of this, one could argue that on the one hand both the starfish and limpet are metaphors for the rejected lover, the 'I' of the poem, and that they offer a contrast to the free and floating smoke which is a metaphor for the loved one, the second person. But it also seems possible that the poet uses the starfish to represent the *Du* and the limpet to represent the *Ich* in order to suggest that both need to be saved by the same force. One could develop this further and argue that while the *Ich* is destined to return to the same spot with every incoming tide, in other words, that it is to relive the experience of rejection time and again, the *Du* will eventually devour the *Ich* and what is more, needs to devour it in order to stay alive.

The stanza that remains in the final version of 'Gwyll' is the middle section of a longer piece which originally consisted of seventeen lines. Kirsch has omitted the opening four lines of the earlier drafts which described the voice of the beloved and the final seven lines which described his skin. In 'Gwyll' as it stands the reader is left with a description of his face and hair. The title in itself symbolizes once more Kirsch's preoccupation with the duality inherent in Nature, for 'Gwyll' is the Welsh (and not Gaelic as stated)[22] word for twilight, the time when night and day meet and where darkness and light weave into each other. Here, as a new day is breaking, the poem creates an atmosphere which is at once beautiful and melancholic. There is something wild and untamed about the lover's beauty. His face is at first compared with the wispy cotton grass, a plant that disintegrates once held (which in its intangibility reminds one of the association between the lover and smoke in 'Caswell Bay'), and then it is compared to the wild orchids, 'Knabenkraut', out on the moor. Language seems inadequate to describe him, for his beauty is greater than that of these plants, and it may be captured in words at best only fleetingly, as fleeting as the glint of the first ray of sunshine on his cheek.

The comparison with these almost intangible entities here again seems to suggest not the transience of the lover's beauty but rather the transience of the poet's possession of it. The moment it is captured, either physically or in words, it is lost. The melancholy brought about by this inability to reach out and hold strikes a sinister chord in the second line of 'Gwyll' as the first element of the compound noun '*Knaben*kraut' coupled with its location, 'im Moor', reminds the reader of the *Schauderballade* 'Der Knabe im Moor', and one cannot overlook the fact that this ballad was written in verse form by Droste-Hülshoff, a poet whose work has often influenced and inspired Kirsch.[23] The Droste-Hülshoff poem relates a young man's ghostly encounters with the 'unselige Spinnerin' on the moor. He is chased through the hostile countryside by 'die verdammte Margaret' and narrowly escapes being buried alive in the moor only through the intervention of his guardian angel. Although the atmosphere in 'Gwyll' is far less eerie than in the Droste-Hülshoff poem which begins: 'O schaurig ist's übers Moore zu gehn / wenn es wimmelt von Heiderauch', it may be significant that in the Droste-Hülshoff poem it is the woman who is damned and it is the young man who is saved by the angel.[24]

The title 'Auflaufendes Wasser Vollmond' creates a magical atmosphere as it sets the scene of this intriguing poem under the light of a full moon. Through the combination of 'Auflaufendes Wasser' with 'Vollmond' it alludes to the forces of nature by which the moon controls the tide and causes the sea to come in to the beach and go out again. In this poem one is reminded of Kirsch's description of Wales as the land of plants, 'Pflanzenland',[25] for the substance of the poem is the poeticization of the shrub spurge. By using the evocative paradox inherent in its German name 'Wolfsmilch' and listing nine different types of spurge she conjures a range of images and emotions. Once more this is a poem which is written from the perspective of an onlooking first person singular who follows and watches a masculine third person. The futility of the act of following him is emphasized as it is described as a pursuit not of a lifetime but of two lifetimes; it is 'he' who always leads and, despite the title's possible allusion to the contrary, as one of the meanings of 'auflaufen' is 'to catch up', the follower never does.

This poem is the only one in the sequence which explicitly refers to the Austrian poet who accompanied Sarah Kirsch on her second visit to Wales. His signet ring with its image of a wolf becomes a symbol of him and by word association the poet is moved to think of the 'Wolfsmilch' (or spurge) which grows in abundance in the woods behind Caswell Bay.[26] The variety of spurge seems to reflect what the poet perceives to be the various aspects of 'his' character, culminating in the ninth variety which is given the Latin botanical term for spurge 'Euphorbia' qualified by the adjective 'austriaca', – a combination which, as far as I can establish, does not refer to an existing type of plant. This imaginary ninth variety is pointedly described as 'bitter'. One might even suggest that the poet's ambivalent attitude towards her companion is reflected in the fact that spurge is a beautiful plant, but that its sap can cause dangerous irritation.

In the final clause the first person is shown to be protective towards the third person, though due to the absence of punctuation it is not clear what protects the third person from the pitfalls which are hidden once the moon disappears. It may be that the 'following' of the second line indicates a caring watchfulness rather than a pursuit, but it is also possible that through searching for the different shrubs the first person will somehow combine them to form a magic formula or recipe to ensure that the third person is kept from falling. It is perhaps worth noting that though the wolf in Kirsch's work is sometimes the traditionally frightening beast (see 'Wir sollen den Weg nicht verlassen [. . .] / sonst / Schnappt uns der Wolf' ['Reisezehrung', *E*, 37]) it is not always the most evil danger. Captivity is a far greater threat: 'Lieber weg in die Berge, selbst wenn man vom Wolf weiß; lieber mit dem eine Nacht kämpfen, als angebunden an einer Stelle' (*LP*, 30). It seems that it is preferable to be in the dangerous company of wolves than to be tied down.

The themes of 'Auflaufendes Wasser Vollmond' are repeated and universalized in 'Seestück' where a less specific picture of a similar situation is painted. The protective attitude of the poetic voice intensifies as it assumes the role of mother: 'Ich bin die / Mutter'. Here again, as in 'Auflaufendes Wasser Vollmond', the first person's actions are significantly *reactions* which are only meaningful in the context of 'the other'; in 'Auflaufendes Wasser Vollmond' the first person singular follows and searches while in 'Seestück' the abandoned mother waits for her sons to return from the sea. The matches in her apron pocket seem to suggest that she will not let her sons out of her reach again once the tide brings them back to the beach. She will burn their boats and tie the men to her apron strings.

'In den Wellen' is another seascape, only this time the first person of the poem is not placed waiting patiently on the seashore, but has waded into the water. The use of the colour green to describe the sea is rich in significance. On the one hand the German 'grün' is associated with immaturity and on the other with hope, a sentiment reinforced in the 'openness' of the sea. This could suggest that the first person is naïve to harbour a hope of catching the fish in the waves. This immature wish is set against the maturity of the summer which is the domain of the second person familiar for whom the poetic voice seems to long as the repetition of 'der Sommer' evokes.

In Kirsch's work the sea is often seen as a hostile element. In 'Landeinwärts' (*Lw*, 146) she declares: 'Lieber lieb ich den / Himmel die graue die schwarze / Luft als das faßbare Meer [. . .]', and in 'Auf einer Klippe' which she recites during the *Entdeckungen* film she writes about the roaring sea: 'Das Meer brüllte im / Wind und übertraf ihn'. In 'Cysteic', too, the sea is a negative element, as it keeps the sons away from the mother, and the suggestion of 'In den Wellen' could be that the first person will only be able to join the 'Du' through drowning in the waves. In 'Spottdrossel' Kirsch returns to an image frequently encountered in her work, namely that of the poet being mocked. One of the main characteristics of the mockingbird is its ability to imitate or mimic other bird-songs, but as its name suggests, the very act of imitating makes it seem as though it is poking fun at the other birds. It is unlikely that Kirsch saw a mockingbird on the Gower and it is more probable that it is through poetic licence that she has transformed the common thrush (*Drossel*) into the more suggestive *Spottdrossel*, and thus the bird's cry, which seems at first to echo the poet's plea, 'Willleben! Willleben!', into a cruel mocking chant and not a sympathetic response to the poet's desperate questions. Other poems which portray the poet as the object of ridicule are 'Auf einer Klippe' (*ET*, 30), where the wind laughs at the poet ('Lachte als er mich / Sah'), and 'Lachen' (*R*, 68) where the tawny owl laughs up his sleeve, again, one assumes at the poet's expense: 'Er lacht sich ins Fäustchen / Weit und breit kein Baum drauf ich sitze / Käuzchen.'

In both 'Wach' (*ET*, 56) and 'Der Mittag' (*E*, 53) another bird, this time the magpie, laughs aloud and in 'Der Mittag' it gets the better of the poet as it steals her earring: 'Laut lacht die Elster sie fällt / Auf meine Schulter sie bettelt / Mirn Ohrring ab [. . .]'. An early example of this theme in her work is in 'Die Probe' (*Z*, 15) where the poet is again striving to possess a 'him' by attempting a mythical task set by an old man. The poet fails and the poem closes with the cruel laughter of the old man: 'Er bog sich / vor Lachen'.

In Kirsch's work, when the birds do not laugh at the poet there is often the sense that their songs carry a meaning, sometimes light-hearted as in 'Die Luft riecht schon nach Schnee' (*R*, 2) where the blackbird is whispering sweet nothings ('Darling flüstert die Amsel'), but more often sinister as in 'Eichen und Rosen' (*K*, 6) ('Böse böse reden schwerverständliche Krähen'). The poet's inability to understand the crows and to elicit an answer from the mockingbird suggest that in both instances the birds conspire against the poet. This is typical of the way birds are portrayed in Kirsch's work where they almost always tease and deceive the poet with their elusiveness, and keep secret their knowledge of the poet's destiny. In one of her best-known poems, 'Der Meropsvogel' (*R*, 37), the reader is again offered a picture of a bird playing tricks on the poet ('Er fliegt doch er sieht / Fliegend zurück, er entfernt sich, nähert sich trotzdem'), and in their collaborative article J. Goheen *et al.* make a similar observation about another poem: '*The Bird*, wählt das Sinnbild der Amsel als Zeichen der Gleichgültigkeit der Natur gegenüber menschlichem Leid'.[27]

The attempts of the poet to communicate with the bird echo a well-known motif in Welsh mythology where in one of the stories of the Mabinogion[28] (with which Sarah Kirsch is familiar) the beautiful Welsh princess, Branwen, captured and imprisoned in Ireland, befriends a starling, teaches it to speak and sends it with a message to her brother, the giant Bendigeidfran, far across the sea to Wales to tell him of her plight and to ask him to come to set her free. The voice in 'Spottdrossel', however, is not successful in communicating with the bird and despite great efforts ('Ich stieg auf ich stieg ab') there is no reward. Unlike the poet the bird is free and can escape from the situation.[29]

The careful use of punctuation – the two exclamation marks in particular and the division between the last two lines which lays emphasis on 'Lachen', as well as the use of 'denn' in the indirect question 'wo denn dein Herz war', add pathos to the poet's plight and the desperate need to find an answer. But the question is never put, for the bird is never caught and the answer will never be known for certain. The tone of this poem, however, as the tone of the other poems written during this second stay in Wales, suggests that the answer is unlikely to be a happy one.

This image of the poet searching for answers in Nature is perhaps a suitable one with which to conclude my observations, for not only is it typical of the Welsh poems but of Kirsch's work as a whole. Time and again Kirsch writes poems which confront the reader with a portrayal of a lonely woman who is either waiting or searching for a lover and who is thus, through her passiveness, not in control of her own destiny. Over decades of writing this theme has lost its adolescent hope which made the dream of revenge possible, and Nature, in its many forms as plants, animals, birds and the elements, has become more and more often a negative force which enjoys the privilege of having insight into the poet's condition whilst keeping the poet ignorant. Since the only poem which shares the secret answers of Nature with the poet belongs to the ones which were discarded by Kirsch,[30] one may be justified in suggesting that for Kirsch there are no answers, only questions, and that as long as there are questions she will continue to write.

Notes

[1] *Entdeckungen: Es riecht nach Tang, Salz und Wahrheit – Sarah Kirsch in Wales*, 13 July 1994, directed by Claus Spahn and Karl Heinz Bahls.

[2] '[. . .], weil ich eigentlich Gedichte schreiben möchte, in denen für den Lesenden noch Spielraum ist, wo er selbst auch etwas machen kann', in Sarah Kirsch, *Erklärungen einiger Dinge* (Ebenhausen bei München, Langewiesche-Brandt, 1978), 13.

[3] Wolfgang Iser, *Der Akt des Lesens: Theorie ästhetischer Wirkung* (Munich, Wilhelm Fink, 1976).

[4] Other notable exceptions to the sombre tone which characterizes so much of Kirsch's poetry include some of the passages in *La Pagerie* and a few other poems mainly in *Erdreich* and *Erlkönigs Tochter* (e.g. 'Was ich in Norwegen lernte', *ET*, 19, and 'Am Walfjord', *ET*, 24). Happiness for Kirsch is usually beyond reach; it is, rather, a state to be longed for and one which is at best temporary. See for example the poem 'Erdrauch', in which she suggests that it is naïve to believe otherwise: 'Und zu verschiedenen Zeiten geschieht es / Daß wir sehr glücklich über / Irgend ein Ding [. . .] / Umhergehen können / [. . .] / So wird es immer sein glauben wir / [. . .] / Wir sind ganz lebendig hüpfen und springen / In den möblierten Wohnungen des Todes' (*E*, 77).

[5] Jürg Amann, *Patagonien. Prosa* (Munich, Piper, 1985), 93.

[6] See, for example, the name 'Frau Martens'.

[7] See the names 'Wendy', 'Suffolk', 'Devil's Dyke'.

[8] See the names 'Elias', 'Franz', 'Maria', 'Edith'.

[9] See the name 'Sascha'.

[10] Kirsch refers to this in the film *Entdeckungen* (see 1 above).

[11] Dylan Thomas, *Collected Poems 1934–1953*, eds. Walford Davies and Ralph Maud (London, Dent, 1988), 134–5.

[12] H. M. Enzensberger, *Museum der modernen Poesie* (Frankfurt am Main, Suhrkamp, 1960). Wulf Kirsten in his article '"Die Welt ist ein Gehöft im Winter"', *Heine Jahrbuch*, 32 (1993), 172–80 draws attention to the important influence of this work on Sarah Kirsch (p. 174).

[13] The striking similarity between the two poems here and the knowledge that, by her own admission, she was already familiar with Dylan Thomas's work makes it difficult to understand how Kirsch can claim in the *Entdeckungen* film that she is surprised by it; referring to her visit she says: 'Das dauerte nur ein paar Tage doch ich schrieb für mich wichtige Texte, die *merkwürdigerweise* mit Dylan Thomas korrespondieren, fast seinen Rhythmus hervorgerufen haben'. (My italics).

[14] See Rhys W. Williams, 'Dylan Thomas' Swansea: Erfindung und Rezeption eines Wunschbilds', in *Literaturen europäischer Küstenregionen* (Kiel, Kulturamt der Stadt Kiel, 1995), 136–43.

[15] Earliest extant articles date from the work of the sixth-century poets Aneirin and Taliesin.

[16] '*Cynghanedd* and English Poetry', *Poetry Wales*, 14 no. 1 (1978), 23–58.

[17] Cf. Martin Kane's article in Chapter Five of this volume about the political meaning hidden behind picture postcard poems.

[18] For a detailed discussion of these poems see Franz Fühmann, 'Gedanken Beim Lesen: Vademecum für Leser von Zaubersprüchen', *Sinn und Form*, 27 (1975), 142–70.

[19] Spottdrossel: Die Braune rief den ganzen Tag / Willeben! Willeben! über den Felsen. / Ich stieg auf ich stieg ab sie zu fragen / Wo denn dein Herz wär. Sie flog / Lachend davon.

[20] For other examples of the omission of the final *n* in Kirsch's work see Roland H. Wiegenstein, 'Approbierte Hexe: Sprechstunden nach Vereinbarung', *Merkur*, 345 (February 1977), 178–84, here 182.

[21] For a treatment of the significance of the shadow in 'Elegie I' see J. Goheen *et al.*, 'Die Optik der Zaubersprüche: Zur Bildpoesie der Sarah Kirsch', *Carleton Germanic Papers*, 29 (1981), 17–40.

[22] See Kirsch's note to the poem in Chapter One of this volume.

[23] Annette von Droste-Hülshoff, 'Der Knabe im Moor', in *Historisch Kritiche Ausgabe: Werke, Briefwechsel*, ed. Winfried Woesler, vol. 1.i, *Gedichte zu Lebzeiten* (Tübingen, Max Niemeyer, 1985), 67–8.

[24] For links with 'Moor', see the poem 'Der Droste würde ich gern Wasser reichen' (Z, 42) which contains the line 'gehn Glucksen übers Moor'; and 'Selbstmord' (Z, 57), which has the line 'Sie wohnten früher am Moor'.

[25] 'Vom Stasiland nach Pflanzenland', *Entdeckungen* (see note 1 above).

[26] One of the discarded poems bears the title of this area, 'Bishop's Wood', and takes its imagery from the Grimm fairy tale of *Brüderchen Schwesterchen* where the deer rather than the wolf is a symbol for the male partner.

[27] J Goheen *et al.*, 'Optik der Zaubersprüche: Zur Bildpoesie der Sarah Kirsch' (see note 21 above).

[28] Readers who are unfamiliar with the tales of the Mabinogion should consult the 1949 translation by Thomas and Gwyn Jones in the Everyman's Library series.

[29] As early as *GS*, 37 this is how Kirsch expresses the wish to be free to escape; 'ach wär ich Vogel, Fluß oder Eisenbahn'. In 'Die Entfernung' (*E*, 26) she turns the adverbial expression 'vogelfrei' into a noun as once more she longs to be free: 'Die Vogelfreiheit entzückte mich'.

[30] This was a poem entitled 'Dritter Spaziergang' which ended with the unhappy liturgy: 'Ich las auf einem Stein der / Freigespült war glückliche / Liebe gibts nie'. And an ironic note here is that the stone is said to be washed free before it reveals its message, as if the only form of freedom on offer is not to escape unscathed with the bird from the hidden dangers of the gorse bush but to realize the pointlessness of pursuing love in the hope of finding happiness as if to suggest that only when one is aware that there is no such thing as happy love, ever, may one be granted some measure of freedom.

9

'Ähnlich stehle ich
mir auch alles zusammen . . .':
Sarah Kirsch's *Das simple Leben*

RHYS W. WILLIAMS

Taking as her inspiration the way in which the starlings appropriate the sounds which surround them, intercutting into their nor-
mal song the 'Treckerlärm, Hundegequietsche und die Kantate
jeweiligen Sonntags aus unserem Fenster' (*SL*, 7), Sarah Kirsch
offers a parallel to the principle of composition which underlies
her own text. It is no coincidence that she entitles this section of
her text 'Kollegen', nor that she employs the term 'Sound' for their
singing, for it has been regularly applied to her own poetry since
Peter Hacks coined the term 'Sarah-Sound'. Her appropriation and
adaptation of the material which surrounds her (radio
programmes, television news, meteorological reports, letters from
colleagues) similarly operates in counterpoint both to passages of
intense lyricism and the banality of daily domestic routines. The
mixture is a beguiling one, and one, moreover, which perplexed,
even irritated the reviewers of her text: Peter Mohr dismisses the
topical references as 'ziemlich wahllos und ohne teifergehende
Reflexionen',[1] while Alexander von Bormann is only slightly less
severe: 'Die Töne werden mit Fleiß gemischt'.[2] By contrast, Hans-
Ulrich Treichel praises the 'Gleichzeitigkeit von politischen
Schreckensereignissen einerseits und dem stoischen und [. . .]
rücksichtslosen Festhalten an der eigenen Arbeit andererseits',[3]
while Joachim Kaiser goes so far as to claim that: 'der sanfte,
unwiderstehliche Sog von Sarah Kirschs gewichtiger Prosa
übertrifft jetzt durchaus die [. . .] ein wenig routiniert wirkende
Kunstfertigkeit ihrer Verse!'[4]
 What is striking about the critical discussion of *Das simple Leben*
is not merely the disparity in the value judgements made by
reviewers, but also the absence of consensus on both the formal
properties and the subject matter of the text. The strength of the
work lies in its carefully modulated antithetical structure. The

oscillation is less between the public events and the private world of Kirsch's rural life in Tielenhemme than between opposing forces of order and entropy, manifest both in the public and the private sphere. On the one hand the text offers images of destruction (violent storms, volcanoes and earthquakes, political upheaval, war and death); on the other a cluster of images and motifs betokening order (farming, gardening, making chutney even, but also creative activity with texts, watercolours and music and positive social intercourse with colleagues, family and friends). While the former destructive elements may predominate, those entropic forces merely demand ever more strenuous efforts on the part of the 'ich'-narrator to counter their depredations. It is in the interest of teasing out the structural balance and illuminating some of the features which critics have hitherto neglected that the current essay has been conceived.

The text consists of 188 sections (if titles are counted as belonging to the following section). The titles of some passages indicate either complete poems, of which ten are included (five of those also appearing in *Erlkönigs Tochter*) or significant passages, seventeen in all, of what might be termed poetic prose. Certain of the latter form separate entries, such as 'Postludium', which appears as a postscript in *Schwingrasen* or the radio talk prefaced 'Guten Morgen!', which recounts appalling suffering under National Socialism. The passages of text thus oscillate between what are clearly diary or notebook entries recalling significant (or, quite frequently, trivial) daily events, and more obviously literary sections. In so far as the entries can be dated, they run from the late summer of 1990 until January 1992. Kirsch's critics have had their problems with dating: Michael Butler above argues that the events are 'a detailed chronicle of a single year – 1991',[5] while Kurt Drawert insists that 'wir haben das 2. Halbjahr des Jahres 1991 vor Augen'.[6] In fact, it is a relatively straightforward task to date some individual entries on the basis of the political and other events which are recorded. The very first entry – 'Kirgisen und Usbeken schlagen sich tot' (*SL*, 5) – permits the reader to date the events as having taken place no earlier than June 1990, when hostilities began. The reference: 'Der Irak fiel in Kuweit ein' (*SL*, 11), points to 2 August 1990; Goethe's birthday (*SL*, 16) to 28 August 1990; Horst Bienek's death (*SL*, 32) to 7 December 1990; the beginning of the land war in the Gulf (*SL*, 48) to 24 February 1991; the Chernobyl anniversary (*SL*, 56) to 26 April 1991; 'Himmelfahrt'

(*SL*, 56) to 9 May 1991, a date given in the text; the attempted coup against Gorbachev (*SL*, 77) to the beginning of August 1991; Ukrainian independence (*SL*, 78) to 14 August 1991; 'Tag der Deutschen Einheit um Gottes willen' (*SL*, 80) to 3 October 1991; the various advent Sundays to December 1991, and the New Year celebrations and Kirsch's journey to view her *Stasi* files to January 1992. For the most part the entries are chronological and were almost certainly intended to be so. Occasionally, the strict chronology is disrupted: the Icelandic poet Steinn Steinarr's birthday (actually 13 October 1990) appears in the August 1990 section (*SL*, 11) and 'Aschermittwoch' (*SL*, 46), which must be 27 March 1991, appears in the middle of a series of references to February 1991. There are possible explanations for these disruptions; both are triggered by verbal association. Pondering the beginning of what was to become the Gulf War and hearing the Hebrides mentioned in a weather report, Kirsch concludes: 'Da möchte ich hin. Als Stein unter Steinen', only to find herself recalling Steinn Steinarr. In the latter case, too, the change is understandable: the verbal association between the beleaguered poet Asher Reich, Kirsch's translator, facing the threat of Scud missile attacks, and Ash Wednesday is a temptation which Kirsch cannot resist: 'Heute ist Aschermittwoch. Ach Asher' (*DSA*, 46). The sense of reading a journal is powerful; Kirsch clearly produces her 'Hefte' with an amalgam of diary entry, personal reminiscence, reflection of public or political issues, and accounts of her travels: she has used much of the latter material for *Spreu*, which concentrated on her public readings and visits abroad from May 1988 to December 1990; with a small overlap of a few months, the current journal takes over.

The opening line – 'Traure meinem vorigen Heft etwas nach' (*SL*, 5) – indicates the opening of a new notebook, though it is clear that Kirsch's literary method is to combine and rewrite earlier notebook entries, retaining phrases and even whole sections which please her. She follows the same 'Methode Gertrud Stein immer wieder von einem ins andere Heft übertragen. Verändern' (*SL*, 45) which she employs for *Spreu*, on which she works during the year period covered by *Das simple Leben*. Readers of *Schwingrasen* will recall another tribute to Gertrud Stein's method,[7] an entry which simultaneously pays tribute to another major influence, namely Robert Walser:

eigentlich schätze ich solche knappen gegenständlicheren Stücke wie
ich seinerzeit *Irrstern* oder was ich später [in *Das simple Leben* RWW]
ausgestanzt habe, etwas das einen Anfang und dann einen Schluß hat,
einen kleinen Aufbau und die gesetzte Spannung – solche Stückchen
wie sie Herr Robert Walser gemacht hat. Robert muß man doch stets
betonen in diesem Lande in dieser Zeit . . . (*Sch*, 34)

It comes as no surprise that Kirsch should pay a further tribute to
Walser in *Das simple Leben*, noting her reading of Walser's *Aus dem
Bleistiftgebiet*, the 'Mikrogramme' which Walser wrote in the years
1924–5 and which were deciphered only in 1985. It would not be
too far-fetched to regard Kirsch's entries as a deciphering of her
own private 'Mikrogramme'.

If I have singled out Gertrude Stein and Robert Walser as
important influences on the structure of Kirsch's text, this is not to
say that they are the only writers who put in an appearance.
Scarcely an entry elapses without some reference to writers,
painters or musicians. The same structural principle of 'gesetzte
Spannung' applies here, too: the writers falling into two main
categories, the one betokening the legitimate attempt to impose an
aesthetic order on the confused experiences of everyday, the other
(chiefly former GDR writers) embodying the very disorder which
must at all costs be countered. To the former group we may allo-
cate both contemporaries and friends of Kirsch: Jiří Gruša, later
appointed Czech ambassador to Germany and to whose poetry
Kirsch is engaged in composing a postscript (*SL*, 8, 19, 29, 32, 38,
55); Asher Reich, who translates her work into Hebrew and whose
fate in an Israel under attack from Saddam Hussein's missiles is a
constant source of her anxiety (*SL*, 29, 38, 46); Herta Müller, the
Rumanian-born novelist whose *Der Teufel sitzt im Spiegel* Kirsch
reads with approbation (*SL*, 66); Inger Christensen (*SL*, 9); Genna
Aigi (*SL*, 9); Ingmar Bergman's autobiography (*SL* 27); Steinn
Steinarr, the Icelandic poet whose birthday is celebrated (*SL*, 11);
the Finnish writer Pentti Saarikoski (*SL*, 17); the Austrian writer
Alfred Kolleritsch (*SL*, 53); the Surinam-born Dutch writer Hans
Faverey (*SL*, 83) and two American writers, Elizabeth Bishop,[8]
whose volume of short stories Kirsch admires (*SL*, 8) and William
Carlos Williams in whose footsteps Kirsch sees herself as treading
(*SL*, 27). Appearing anonymously as the 'Engel welcher aus
Salzburg eingeschwebt war' (*SL*, 50) is the Austrian poet
Christoph W. Aigner, whose drawings adorn the cover of the

text.[9] What is striking about the constellation of authors who are mentioned positively, is that none was born in Germany; it is as if Sarah Kirsch were consciously inventing a non-German canon, as if German writers were too caught up in the destructive German–German debates to be accorded the positive ordering function which Kirsch demands of literature.

When we turn to those German authors who are mentioned, it is equally striking that virtually all are products of the former GDR. They fall into two clear categories: those who, like Kirsch herself, left the GDR in the aftermath of the Biermann expulsion, a group viewed positively; and those who elected to stay and who become the object of Kirsch's scorn and vituperation. West German authors are noticeable only by their absence. To the ex-GDR writers presented more positively belong Erich Loest, whose televised return to Leipzig is documented (*SL*, 6); Bernd Jentzsch pays a visit in a dream (*SL*, 27); Horst Bienek's death is recorded (*SL*, 32); the documentary account of Günter Kunert's *Stasi* files prompt Kirsch's despairing outburst: 'Die Willfährigkeit der Menschen aber zur Denunziation haut einem die Füße glatt weg' (*SL*, 34); and the resignation of both Kunert and Reiner Kunze from the West Berlin Academy of Arts under protest at the unification of the two Academies is noted with apparent approval (*SL*, 91); Uwe Kolbe also pays a visit to Tielenhemme (*SL*, 56). The writers of the GDR who remained in the country after 1976 are roundly condemned for having compromised their position. At the very beginning of the text Kirsch orders from a bookshop a copy of Christa Wolf's *Was bleibt*, to which title she erroneously adds a question mark (*SL*, 8). Kirsch's views on the text are not recorded, but her reaction to the television film 'Zeitschleifen' is unequivocal: 'Frau Lupus [Christa Wolf] verglich sich mit Anna Achmatowa die auch viel Unbill hinnehmen mußte. Gerade fiel mein Schuh neben den Fernseher noch' (*SL*, 56). One suspects that her own text 'Lachstreifen' (*SL*, 38) is conceived as a sardonic counter-measure to the Wolf film. Reflecting on this group of writers, Kirsch observes: 'Charlie zum Beispiel und Volker und auch noch andere aber nicht alle die im Lande blieben in diesem engen Vater-Haus, sie haben immer noch die Hausgötter in Kopp. Brecht & Co. welche sie bedienen müssen. Das hindert doch auf die Dauer. Sie sitzen in ihrer eigenen Tinte' (*SL*, 33). The gradual revelation of the extent of *Stasi* surveillance and the way in which writers' groups were infiltrated emerges only gradually. The

discovery that Sascha Anderson (whom Kirsch rechristens Sascha
Stasisohn) was a *Stasi* operative, an *IM*, does not seem to surprise
Kirsch, though her friend Elke [Elke Erb] has the greatest diffi-
culty in comprehending the betrayal (*SL*, 67 and 81). Further dis-
closures follow: the brother of Schott [Hans Joachim Schädlich]
was also an informant, under the cover-name 'Schäfer' (a name
which, placed alongside Kirsch's own practical involvement with
sheep in this text, acquires a dreadful irony).[10] For Kirsch, these
discoveries merely confirm the corrupt nature of a system which
she detested: 'Wer von den Künstlern sich beim Gedanken an die
Stasi gleich in die Hosen machte der ging in die Höhle des Löwen
und bot seine Dienste da an. [. . .] In keinem anderen
Ostblockland aber hatte ein Geheimdienst so viele freiwillige
Helfer wie hier' (*SL*, 90). It is only when Kirsch is granted access
to her own *Stasi* files in January 1992 that a genuine sense of
shock and despair emerges, swiftly followed, a day or so later, by
outrage and then relief: 'War in mein früheres Leben glatt
rückversetzt. Weil noch jeder belanglose Anruf nachzulesen da
war. [. . .] Meine rückgespulte Biographie war reine Menschen-
kunde. OV "Milan" von Freund Feind und IM "Verleger"
verraten' (*SL*, 88); 'Heute geht es mir besser. Es regte das frühere
Leben mich auf. Das Ländchen es hat mich geknebelt und
schickaniert. Ich kann alles bloß in die Entfernung rücken und
mich immer wieder beglückwünschen daß ich mit Moses entkam'
(*SL*, 89).

   Das simple Leben provides ample evidence that her experiences
in the GDR have never left Sarah Kirsch. Throughout the text, the
GDR continues to provoke extreme reactions; it is almost as if the
landscape of Schleswig-Holstein and daily life in Tielenhemme are
defined *ex negativo* by their contrast to the GDR. Kirsch appears
unable to delight in the here and now of Tielenhemme without
first defining it as the counterpoint to a GDR world. The commis-
sion to write an article on the German–German situation is the
first indication of the highly articulate scorn which she pours on
the 'Ländchen'; visits from Julchen, the 'Jugendgespielin aus
Halftown' [Halberstadt], again conjure up memories of childhood,
but the occasion also unleashes 'seltsame Träume, die sämtlich in
der Vergangenheit spielten' (*SL*, 14). But Kirsch is swift to repudi-
ate any suggestion of sympathy for the GDR in its current plight,
preferring to show her visitors the sights of Schleswig-Holstein
rather than dwell on 'das zerbrechende ehemalige Ländchen'. A

visit to Greifswald serves to unite her rejection of the GDR with her sensitivity to the environment: 'Vorgestern also nach Greifswald wo die Fische im Bodden hautlos ja schwimmen. Dank AKWs. Furchtbare Dörfer gesehen. Wohn- und Schweinebaracken nicht unterscheidbar. [. . .] Die Städte zum Weinen' (*SL*, 20–1). When Julchen leaves Tielenhemme Kirsch notes that the journey will take eleven hours 'weil ihre Reichsbahn so verrottet ja ist' (*SL*, 77). While the landscape of Kirsch's childhood still retains its attraction it cannot counterbalance the psychological pressure which the GDR continues to impose:

> Bin sehr froh aus dem Ländchen wieder entfernt zu sein. Es war dort barbarisch, nur die großen Landschaften zwischen Halle und Leipzig und Leipzig und Göttingen lachten mich an. [. . .] Wie die Seele in Ossiland sich malträtiert fühlt. Dagegen muß ich anfluchen. (*SL*, 80)

The only adequate response to the GDR, for Kirsch, remains vehement and violent rejection; yet the imprecations which she hurls betray an emotional involvement from which even the attractions of a rural idyll cannot distract.

While the many references to the GDR give *Das simple Leben* a political dimension, its topicality is ensured by the frequent news items which punctuate the text. War rumbles on in the background: in the Caucasus, in the Gulf, and in the Balkans. It is difficult to discern any partisanship in Kirsch's reactions to conflict. While it is clear that she opposes all manifestations of war, commenting sympathetically on the anti-war demonstrations in Germany, her sympathies are aroused when the state of Israel is threatened. She records signing a pro-Israeli letter for the *Frankfurter Allgemeine Zeitung*, and goes to some lengths to secure for her son an Israeli flag for his demonstration. There are echoes here of her much earlier battle against the anti-Semitism of her father and her decision to adopt the name Sarah – she was born Ingrid Bernstein – out of solidarity with persecuted German Jews. There is even a suggestion that her father may have had Jewish ancestry which he was, perhaps understandably under National Socialism, anxious to deny.[11] Yet for the most part her response is detached; war is opposed because it threatens friends, such as Asher; or because it threatens to pollute still further an ever more polluted world. Kirsch does not engage with the Gulf War debate. The logical consequence of her support for Israel is opposition to the Iraqi regime, but she fights shy of such a conclusion. There is also a hint of support for Gorbachev, as the coup attempt is reported, but that support is more easily projected into one of her son's friends. World politics do obtrude upon her consciousness, but their significance is relativized by juxtaposition with the more mundane elements of life in the country and private concerns.

If war represents the unleashing of destructive forces in human affairs, then storms, volcanoes and earthquakes represent their counterparts in the natural world. Often these complexes are causally connected: war produces the oil pollution which will, in turn, affect weather conditions; but even where the connections are more tenuous, associative links emerge from the juxtaposition of passages. The book begins with natural disaster: 'Erdbeben und Vulkane in diesem Jahr' (*SL*, 5); and it is with disaster that it ends: 'Vulkanausbruch auf den Philippinen' (*SL*, 64); 'Über Nacht hat es im Kölner Raum ein Erdbeben gegeben' (*SL*, 98); and, the last words of the text: 'Der Ätna speit' (*SL*, 99). The global threat of pollution through oil and radioactivity is ever-present: in the section entitled 'Federgewand' an oil slick has killed a drake and will soon account for its mate: 'Es fällt mir in solchem Moment eine unglaubliche Wut auf die parasitären Menscher und die Zustände des Planeten glatt an' (*SL*, 23–4). The anniversary of the Chernobyl disaster brings a television report on the surrounding villages, abandoned and uninhabitable since the accident; Kirsch notes the 'Dornröschen-Effekt', the sense of everyday human activity held in suspended animation, then relates it to the volcanoes with which the text opens and closes with the laconic: 'Pompei' (*SL*, 56).

Apart from its wider association with the 'Katastrophismus' which characterizes the literature of the 1980s and early 1990s, the weather forms a substantial part of Kirsch's text. In its destructive phase it is associated with death: 'Im Sturm höre ich Stimmen: menschliches Geschimpfe viel Klagen. Das werden irgendwelche Ertrunkenen sein' (*SL*, 18); not infrequently, storms signal, through a kind of 'pathetic fallacy', cataclysmic upheavals in the affairs of men. Just such a disturbance opens the volume: the writer's anxiety about embarking on a new project is associated with civil unrest in the Caucasus, with violence in nature, and with the death of the blacksmith. Storm seems to be the natural element in Tielenhemme, for the third section of the text is taken over verbatim from the volume *Schwingrasen*, where it appears under the title 'Lachen':

> Um vom Sturm etwas zu begreifen oder gar vermitteln zu können, muß man an der Grenze zwischen Wasser und Land angestammt sein, dort wo er sich auf die Welt wirft, frisch und ungebrochen direkt aus dem Äther . . . (*SL*, 5–6)

Not only is Sarah Kirsch making a fairly obvious point about the significance of weather for a rural and coastal community, she is also situating herself on the edge, as it were, on a 'Grenze' between land and sea, a 'Grenze' which is simultaneously one between creativity and destruction, between order and chaos.

It is not merely international politics which unleashes destructive forces; nature, too, supplies its volcanoes and earthquakes. Yet the threat posed by natural forces is not restricted to the spectacular eruption; insidious forces are silently at work in the surrounding marshland. The landscape of Tielenhemme itself is a threatened one, in need of constant human intervention to render it habitable: 'Würden die Gräben nicht aller zwei Jahre sorgfältig ausgehoben, so wäre hier alles verloren' (*SL*, 30). Even in times of good weather subversive forces are operating: 'Ne kräftige Natur waltet in diesen Sümpfen' (*SL*, 33). Indeed, so threatened is the landscape by the encroachment of the marsh, that young people are abandoning their farms in the area and are moving east into the former GDR of all places, where agricultural land is cheaper. The farming and gardening undertaken by Kirsch is an attempt to hold back these forces, much as her text itself, despite its fragmentary nature, seeks to structure and order in antithetical form her potentially destructive emotions.

A recurrent feature of *Das simple Leben* is the inclusion of meteorological reports from the weather station at Mariehamn. In *Schwingrasen*, in the section 'Seewetterbericht' (*Sch*, 37–41), Kirsch illustrates the poetic power which the weather reports have for her, setting free the 'Kino im Kopf' of her imagination.[12] What is made explicit in the earlier piece is present only by implication in *Das simple Leben*: here the weather reports are presented factually; we surmise only that they similarly release the imagination: 'Höre den Seewetterbericht und bleibe in Mariehamn wiederum hängen' (*SL*, 14). The reports (*SL*, 11, 14, 30, 43, 54, 58) offer public, factual, scientific accounts of the weather, counterbalancing the more

private reactions to storm and sunshine which accompany so
many of the notebook entries. That the Mariehamn reports are
carefully and evenly distributed throughout the text suggests that
they, too, provide a structural framework. The weather is not
simply an arbitrary backcloth to the human events; it determines
much of the human activity and is, in turn, affected by human
activity. Structurally, the weather pulls together many of the
recurrent motifs. The storm is related to the recurrent preoccupation with death, reinforced by the apparently casual remark:
'Großer Gott wir ersaufen ja wiederum gleich' (*SL*, 20); it necessi-
tates repair work to the garden, symbolizing the struggle of order
against the tendency to disorder; and it echoes political upheaval
through 'Operation Wüstensturm' (*SL*, 40).

The images of destruction conveyed both by storms and political upheaval find their clearest expression in the preoccupation
with death. The tone is set at the beginning of the text by the
death of the local blacksmith; the wind in the grass suggests the
whispering of drowned sailors, a fate which Kirsch and her com-
panions escape on their expedition only because they press on
over the mud-flats, defying the incoming tide: 'An Umkehr war
nach einer bestimmten Entfernung nicht zu denken, es wäre der
sichere Tod nun gewesen' (*SL*, 12). Apart from the dead in the
Gulf War and the birds killed by oil pollution, Kirsch
'weichgeklopft von schimmernden Todesgedanken' (*SL*, 26), registers 'Todes Hauch der durch den Raum wie durch alles übrige
fliegt' (ibid.). Later she reports that 'heute ist dieser bei mir sehr
beliebte Todten-Sonntag' (*SL*, 30). Death obtrudes, moreover, on
those activities which Kirsch more usually associates with counter-
ing destructiveness: her activity on the small-holding and her
creative work. Jonathan, one of her sheep, dies; and her writer
colleagues, too, are celebrated through their deaths: Elizabeth
Bishop, who possesses the writer's skill 'Tote zum Leben
erwecken' (*SL*, 8), is herself 'längst tot' (ibid.); Kirsch mourns both
the Finnish poet Pentti and Horst Bienek, and she discovers for
herself the writing of Hans Faverey, who died the previous year:
in his work she finds 'alles über den Tod. Ohne mit der Wimper
zu zucken' (*SL*, 83). As if taking her cue from Faverey, Kirsch
adopts a strikingly matter-of-fact tone in her references to death;
at the same time death is ever-present, outweighing by some margin more hopeful experiences, such as the birth of a calf. Images
of death are often juxtaposed with more light-hearted observation,

or ironized by the use of antiquated language or the employment of pet names for the animals; but the wind continues to whisper of drowned sailors.

The self-referentiality of Kirsch's prose texts has been presented both as a defect and a strength. References to family, pets, farm animals, friends and colleagues, sometimes disguised with more or less easily decipherable pet names, has aroused irritation: Moritz, Kirsch's son, appears under his own name in *Spreu*, but is disguised as Moses (or 'Wasserbaby') in *Das simple Leben*. Kirsch's world becomes, after a confusing start (for the distinction between humans and animals only gradually emerges), a familiar one to the reader: Ambrosius the composer, Loulou, Anna Blume, Peter der Große, and Wassilij the cats, Schumann the dog, Bosch the donkey, Cleopatra the tortoise, not to mention, by name at least, all the sheep. There is, of course, a danger of mawkish sentimentality about Kirsch's desire to impose familiarity on her domestic world by naming it; but critics have been slow to realize that Kirsch has a serious purpose. Her anything but simple life is, like her creative writing, an attempt at ordering, not dissimilar to her efforts to name birds, fish and flowers by their correct biological and botanical names. As the German Romantics illustrated, the use of a name confers a peculiar power over nature; within the universe of Kirsch's circumscribed domestic sphere, she may impose her vision (and, as the names for the most part suggest, that vision is an artistic one). She is seeking, one could argue, to transform her world into an aesthetic construct, yet is aware, simultaneously, of the impossibility of her task. The urgency of that task is conditioned by the destructive forces which she observes around her. If the naming appears excessively twee or sentimental, it is because it has to counter peculiarly insidious external forces. In a book in which Kirsch recounts with ill-concealed despair her confrontation with her own *Stasi* files, files which reveal the full extent of the way in which her personal privacy was invaded by malign intrusive forces, her need to construct a counter model of order could scarcely be more insistent. The naming of the animals may be viewed – more charitably than many critics have been prepared to do – as a counterblast to the 'Decknamen' employed by the *Stasi*. At a time in the history of the Federal Republic when there was a national obsession with naming names, Kirsch's playful inventions are the more understandable. *Das simple Leben* offers a brief history and taxonomy of

a certain kind of artistic sensibility. In granting the reader carefully controlled insight into her private world, Kirsch is setting
limits to what might otherwise be an intrusive preoccupation with
her private life, but simultaneously she is supplying her own
personal and carefully orchestrated version of it.

Kirsch's use of private spellings and quasi-baroque for-
mulations also suggests an attempt on her part to ironize
experiences and events. Her orthography is not consistent. On
occasions she adopts contracted forms of the indefinite article ('ne'
for 'eine', 'isses' for 'ist es', and 'wien' for 'wie ein') rather in the
manner of Arno Schmidt. The effect is to give certain passages a
conversational tone, a casual intimacy with the reader appropriate
to the diary form; such passages contrast sharply with more
essayistic passages with orthodox spelling and punctuation. Some
spellings suggest private jokes: 'qu' appears always as 'kw'
('Akwarelle', 'kwehr', 'Kwantum', 'kwalmte') and 'chs'
occasionally as 'x' ('wäxt', 'nix', 'überwexeln'), like a private
suggestion for spelling reform. Other forms point to a kind of
false historicizing: 'diesz', 'werth', 'Morgenroth', 'Insul', 'Articul',
'corrigierte'. Employed relatively rarely, these forms again suggest
a playful, ironic distancing, which helps to explain why they are
used most frequently of experiences connected with the GDR
(which is itself denoted, characteristically, by 'DDDR' or 'das
Ländchen'). It is as if Kirsch cannot bring herself to speak of the
GDR and her experiences without recourse to ironic distancing.
Here, it is linguistic ingenuity which offers a counterweight to
destructive experience.

Critics have noted that this text supplies a history of the incep-
tion of three works: *Spreu*, *Schwingrasen* and *Erlkönigs Tochter* (at
least as far as some of the earlier poems are concerned). Kirsch
offers sometimes tantalizing glimpses into her literary and artistic
methods, her discussions with her publisher's reader, her attention
to details of cover design, and her method of transcription.
Among the most interesting of these reflections is one which is
devoted to her poetry readings. While making no bones about the
need to earn money, she is aware of the problematic relationship
between the immediate inspiration of her poetry, the
reconstitution of the poem through its being read, and the likely
contextual interpretation on each occasion. Recalling a reading
tour the previous spring, she notes that the poem alluded to birds,
to a shower of rain starting to fall, and to a door banging in the

wind. As she reads, reconstructing in her mind the situation which inspired her poem, she is aware that the door in the room where the reading is taking place, has also slammed. The poem in question may be identified as 'Anfang März' from the collection *Schneewärme*:

> Tag der Brachvögel die als
> Himmlische Töne von der
> Arbeit ablenken. [. . .]
>
> Und schön ist auch das
> Geräusch des einfallenden
> Warmen Regens im Frühjahr [. . .]
>
> Und es klappert im Wind
> Die lebendige Hoftür . . . . (*SW*, 58)

Kirsch is aware that 'jeder Augenblick ist absolut' (*SL*, 25), but is charmed by the coincidence. The birdsong in the poem is clearly the 'absolute' moment, permanently fixed in her poetic universe; it is not subject to decay or disruption; if another bird is heard while the poem is being read, the coincidence may be enjoyed, but the existence of the song within the poem can never be called into question. It is not subject to the vagaries of chance, nor to the changing nature of Kirsch's audiences. Self-referentiality here is not a private game so much as a reassertion of the independence from time and place of the poem itself. There are, of course, in the prose echoes of poetry which has emerged, or is to emerge in future, from the notebook entries. One example will suffice: a late entry reads:

> Um fünf Uhr sitze ich schon wieder am Schreibtisch. Sternlos die Nacht und bibelschwarz. Sehr widersätzliches Material. Meingott es wird auch immer schwerer. Man erhascht ein Splitterchen vor alles versinkt. (*SL*, 97)

Readers of *Erlkönigs Tochter* will spot the allusion in 'sternlos und bibelschwarz' to the opening lines of Dylan Thomas's *Under Milk Wood* and will note that the line reappears, appropriately enough, in the poem 'Mumbles Bay' (*ET*, 38). This poem, then, appears to be the difficult material on which Kirsch is working. Curiously another line from the same poem appears, in a quite different context, in *Spreu*. Sailing north to Sweden in January 1990, Kirsch is woken by a raging storm: 'Bin unersättlich ins Wasser zu starren wenn der Sturm Trichter und Treppen und eisige Schneisen tief in das Meer wühlt' (*S*, 65). The words reappear in 'Mumbles Bay' as:

> Der Sturm
> Riß Trichter und Treppen eisige Schneisen
> Tief in das Meer . . . (*ET*, 39)

The alliteration suggests more the rhythms of Germanic or Norse poetry than Dylan Thomas and its original context gives a clue as to what was in Kirsch's mind. But clearly she felt that the line was too good to discard and could be readily transposed from the Baltic to the Irish Sea. *Das simple Leben* offers the reader some clues to the genesis of some of Kirsch's other prose works and poems. For the Germanist it may well constitute a valuable source of information, but it must be used with caution. Despite the text's journal-like quality, despite its apparent autobiographical relevance, it is a product of the literary imagination. While it offers illuminating insights into Kirsch's mental processes, its use of recurrent motifs, its structural patterns, and its consistent thematic focus, make it a work of more general interest than merely a guide-book to the geography of Sarah Kirsch's poetic world.

It has been remarked upon that Kirsch has published in recent years more prose than poetry[13] and perhaps a reading of *Das simple Leben* will help to explain why. Despite the overall consistency of her thematic concerns, if one compares her early poetry from the GDR with her last two collections, one is struck by how much more minimalist her poetry has become; the poetic tone, the 'Sound', remains unaltered, but the reader is given less and less help. The prose works are more accessible; they can articulate in more differentiated fashion the complexities of contemporary experience, the tensions between destructive forces and an ordered universe. Political and social concerns, which Kirsch has, since her departure from the GDR, largely excised from her poetry, can reappear in the prose works without threatening the 'absolute' nature of poetic utterance. There is more room in her prose for reflection, for paradox, for opinion and for untidy emotions like anger and the struggle to control it; the poems represent the distillation of what emerges after the primary process has taken place.

Das simple Leben both presents and embodies a process of ordering, an ultimately vain attempt to counter the disorder which constantly threatens; such solutions as are possible are merely temporary: after the ditches are cleared, after the dikes are repaired, new depredations will inevitably follow. Each text, each poem, is but a temporary victory. Where the pressures are overwhelming, where they threaten the personality, the efforts to counter them may appear shrill or forced, but, in Kirsch's own words 'Man muß dagegen anleben was natürlich blendend gelingt. Mir' (*SL*, 27).

Notes

[1] Peter Mohr, 'Tiefenströmung "haut uns die Füße weg"', *Rheinische Post*, 16 April 1994. A shortened version of Mohr's review, under the even less charitable title 'Zuviel Akwawitt', appeared in the *General-Anzeiger* on 28–29 May 1994.

[2] *Frankfurter Rundschau*, 19 July 1994.

[3] *Der Tagesspiegel*, 26 June 1994.

[4] 'Kleines Meisterwerk und größere Hoffnung', *Süddeutsche Zeitung*, 17 March 1994.

[5] See above, 53.

[6] *Die Weltwoche*, 31 March 1994. Dorothea von Törne in *Literatur*, 9 March 1994, is right to speak of the 'Tagesschau der Jahre 1990 bis 1992'.

[7] *Schwingrasen*, 34.

[8] It is feasible that Bishop's poetry has also served as inspiration for Kirsch. One of her most admired poems from the collection *Geography III* of 1976 – see Elizabeth Bishop, *The Complete Poems 1927–1979* (London, Chatto & Windus, 1974), 162–6 – is 'Crusoe in England', which may have inspired Kirsch's poem 'Crusoe' (see *Bodenlos*, 48), as well as her decision to entitle her 1995 anthology *Ich Crusoe*. Bishop's sensitivity to place and landscape displays many of the features also found in Kirsch's work.

[9] It seems likely that Kirsch's lavish tribute to a fellow writer (*SL*, 78–9) refers also to Aigner.

[10] For a discussion of his reactions to his *Stasi* files, see Hans Joachim Schädlich (ed.), *Aktenkundig* (Reinbek bei Hamburg, Rowohlt, 1993). Kirsch supplies for this publication four poems, one of which is 'Die andere Welt' from *Das simple Leben*.

[11] See Hans Wagener, *Sarah Kirsch* (Berlin, Kolloquium, 1989), 5–6.

[12] For a poetic version, see 'Marienhamn' in *Erlkönigs Tochter*, 35.

[13] See Michael Butler's article in Chapter Seven of this volume.

10

Erinnerungen

HEINZ LUDWIG ARNOLD

Ich habe Sarah Kirsch erstmals in Göttingen getroffen, bald nach ihrem Übertritt in den Westen, den sie mit der ihr eigenen Kraft und Resolutheit durchsetzte, aus dem 17. Stockwerk jener Mammutbauten auf der Ost-Berliner Fischerinsel nach West-Berlin. Ich hatte sie zu einer Lesung nach Göttingen eingeladen, ins überfüllte Auditorium des Deutschen Theaters, und nach der Lesung versanken wir im Bordeaux. Seither, so denke ich, sind wir befreundet und teilen uns Freude und Ärger mit.

Damals kannte ich nur ihren zweiten Gedichtband: *Zaubersprüche* von 1973, und erinnerte aus dem Gedicht »Besinnung« die rebellischen Zeilen:

> Was bin ich für ein vollkommener weißgesichtiger Clown
> Am Anfang war meine Natur sorglos und fröhlich
> Aber was ich gesehen habe zog mir den Mund
> In Richtung der Füße. (Z, 43)

Damals hatte die Besinnung wohl auch eingesetzt nach Arbeiten, die Sarah Kirsch auf Materialsuche erneut in die Wirklichkeitserfahrung geführt hatten – aus der sie ja kam nach dem Abitur mit ihrer Arbeit in einer Fabrik und einem abgeschlossenen Studium der Biologie –; in *Die Pantherfrau* hatte sie 1973, im Jahr der »Zaubersprüche«, Texte versammelt, sozialen und beruflichen Verhältnisse von fünf Frauen nachgeforscht, Texte, die sie »Romanextrakte« genannt hat. Sieht man sie, von heute her, zusammen mit den gleichzeitig erschienenen ersten Erzählungen in dem Band *Die ungeheuren bergehohen Wellen auf See*, so kann man mutmaßen, daß nach maßgeblichen lyrischen Arbeiten Sarah Kirsch auf der Suche nach neuen Artikulationsformen war – zur Prosa hin, freilich kaum zur sozialistisch realistischen.

Doch daraus wurde – einstweilen – nichts.

Ihre »Zaubersprüche« hat Sarah Kirsch damals Gedichte genannt, »die sich aus einer Gelegenheit entfalten«: Gedichte also,
die nicht nur Empfindungen beschreiben, umsetzen in Stimmung
aus Wort und Tönung, sondern die, indem sie aus den Gelegenheiten wachsen, auch die *Ursachen* der Empfindungen enthalten
und abbilden, freilich verschlüsselt, eingezogen in das Zusammen-
spiel von Klängen, Farben und Bildern. Das gilt, variantenreich,
bis heute.

Noch eines sei der Erinnerung geschuldet: Aus dem nächsten
Gedichtband, dem letzten in der DDR erschienenen: *Rückenwind*,
hat Sarah Kirsch damals in Göttingen gelesen: Liebesgedichte,
Naturgedichte: aus Gelegenheiten und bei Gelegenheiten entstan-
dene Gedichte von meist zarten Stimmungen. Pastelltöne, keine
grellen Farben und Bilder; dennoch sind diese Gedichte keine
Idyllen – im Gegenteil. Wo die Idylle erscheint, Ursache vielleicht
einer gelegentlichen Stimmung, wie im Gedicht »Ende Mai«:

> Du schick die leichteste
> Aller Tauben windförmig sie bringt
> Ungeöffnet tagschnelle Briefe. Schatten
> Unter den Augen; mein wüster Herzschlag (*R*, 4)

– wo also Idyllik aufzukommen scheint, folgt bald darauf der
Gegensatz: da wird die Idylle, abstrakt wie die leichteste aller
Tauben über der Wirklichkeit schwebend, zerstört vom Blick, der
unter dem schönen Schein eine idyllenlose Wirklichkeit erkennt
und zu ihr hin drängt; denn weiter heißt es in diesem Gedicht:

> Unfroh seh ich des Laubs grüne Farbe, verneine
> Bäume Büsche und niedere Pflanzen: ich will
> Die Blätter abflattern sehen und bald. Wenn mein Leib
> Meine nicht berechenbare Seele sich aus den Stäben
> Der Längen- und Breitengrade endlich befreit hat. (*R*, 4)

Oder auch umgekehrt wird Wirklichkeit benannt, um von vor-
neherein den Schein des Idyllischen, der entstehen könnte im
Anblick von Natur, ursächlich zu zerstören:

> Ein Bauer mit schleifendem Bein
> Ging über das Kohlfeld, schwenkte den Hut
> Als wäre er fröhlich. (*R*, 47)

Nur ein ganz kurz angeleuchtetes Bild, voller Lakonie, in dem der
Prozeß von Sehen, Fühlen, Denken und Erkennen im Moment
konzentriertester Wirkung festgehalten ist.

Das Gedicht Sarah Kirschs, soviel wenigstens noch, vermeidet
dabei bewußt den großen lyrischen Gestus; das liest man schon
den Titeln ab: *Sommergedichte – Wintergedichte – Katzenkopfpflaster –
Drachensteigen – Wind – Schatten – Erdreich – Zwischen Herbst und
Winter – Katzenleben – Landwege – Luft und Wasser – Schneewärme –
Die Flut –* samt und sonders Titel, die Zeiten und Orte in der
Natur benennen und ab den 80er Jahren auch viel mit ihrem Le-
ben auf dem schleswigholsteinischen Lande zu tun haben – sogar
Erlkönigs Tochter mag im Nebel an der Eider sich bilden.

Prosa hat Sarah Kirsch nach der *Pantherfrau* und den *Ungeheuren bergehohen Wellen auf See* lange Zeit nicht veröffentlicht – bis
1980 ein Bändchen mit Prosatexten erschien, *La Pagerie*: kurze
Notate nach einem sommerlichen Aufenthalt in einem alten
verfallenden provençalischen Schlößchen – Texte, die Stimmungen
evozieren, nicht beschreiben; leichte, helle, eben sommerliche
Texte, deutlich Prosa, weder Vorstufen zu Gedichten noch lyrische
Prosa:

> Im Schloßhof stehen die weißen Tische, sitzen die Stühle mit ihren rosa
> Pfefferminzplätzchenkissen, Licht wird verschwendet. Das Hündchen
> liegt da als ein Bettvorleger, knurrt und stinkt. Grünes Pergament in
> den Bäumen, jedes Blatt mit über dreißig Zipfelchen. (*P*, 31)

Sechs Jahre später folgte neuerlich ein Band mit Prosatexten:
Irrstern. Darin dieser: »Nebel«:

> Mitte des achten Monats während ich Wolle am Brunnen wasche kann
> ich meine Füße nicht mehr erkennen und lange das Haus nicht das ich
> verließ. Alte Weiber setzt man ins Moor aus Kiebitze hüten sie rufen
> mit verschimmelten Stimmen immer gegen den Wind und gehen
> allmählich verloren. Die Nächte werden länger die Träume dunkler
> und allenthalben stürzen Flugzeuge Bewohner des Irrsterns herunter in
> unwegsame Gebirge. (*I*, 40)

Nicht nur ihre Stimmung unterscheidet diese Texte von jenen
aus *La Pagerie*. Vor allem sind die sprachlichen Mittel die sie nun
hervorrufen, andere: Der Blick des sprechenden Ich, samt all seinen Sinnen, geht nicht nur über die wahrnehmbare Fläche der
Gegenstände, Landschaft, Tiere und Menschen sondern richtet

sich auch nach Innen, holt Erinnerung herein, spinnt Gedankenfäden weiter, wird mehrschichtig, dem Geschauten verbindet sich
Gedachtes und Erahntes, und dies oft wie im Traum mit seiner
ganz eigenen Grammatik. Etwa so:

> Zu große aufgepustete Drosseln in der schwarzen nach Nordost
> geneigten Allee bis der Milchwagen später als sonst die Reise beginnt
> das Tuckern des Treckers lange zu hören ist gar nicht zur Ruhe
> gelangen kann immer wieder in der blitzenden Luft hängt von Einöde
> zu Einöde schwingt sich am Mittag verdoppelt wenn der Trecker zu-
> rückkehrt mit sorglosen pfeifenden Kannen. (I, 8)

Man mache eine kleine Übung mit einem anderen kurzen Text,
der »Trost« überschrieben ist und weder Punkt noch Komma hat;
er kommt geheimnisvoll daher:

> Aber das macht nichts je früher desto besser im Sommer ist Sommer
> später fällt dir der kleine Zahn Träume von Zähnen betreffen Ver-
> wandtschaft einfach so hin ins Gras (I, 59)

Der Text, wie gesagt, endet ohne Punkt, endet also wohl nicht,
geht weiter, aber wie? Wer mag aufheben, was da so ins Gras
fällt? Und was fällt da? »der kleine Zahn«? Jedenfalls auch etwas,
das aus einem Traum stammen kann.

Und die Satzteile davor? »Aber das macht nichts« – »je früher
desto besser« – »im Sommer ist Sommer«: Trostsprüche, so dahin-
gesagte, Banalitäten? Das kann man ja auch anders lesen: »Aber
das macht nichts. Je früher desto besser im Sommer. Ist Sommer
später fällt dir [. . .]«. Oder auch der Satz »Je früher desto besser
im Sommer ist Sommer. Später fällt [. . .]« – ist denkbar. Das läßt
sich, nicht gerade beliebig, aber immer spielerischer fortsetzen:
Denkbares wird evoziert, Phantasie in Gang gesetzt – Leser mobi-
lisiert Eure Träume!

Auch der Satz aus dem Text »Drosseln« steht in einer Sprache
bzw. Grammatik, die unterschiedliche Wahrnehmungen ineinand-
erzieht oder überlagert, deshalb der Phantasie unterschiedliche
Lesarten bereitstellt: Während das formulierende beobachtende
phantasierende – träumende? – Ich die Drosseln in der Allee und
den Milchwagen sieht, hört es das – penetrante? – Tuckern des
Treckers; und dann wird aus dieser ziemlich »normalen« Beschreibung ein polyphoner Text bzw. Vorgang, wie er in solcher Über-
lagerung auch in Träumen begegnet. Wollte man die Grammatik

solcher *Traum*sprache im *Wach*zustand in Sprache setzen, könnte sie wohl in solcher Transkription der meisten Texte aus *Irrstern* erscheinen.

Die Landschaft auch dieser Texte liegt im Norden, am Rande eines Dorfes – und eben im Inneren des vermittelnden Ich. Doch Idyllen wollen da nicht entstehen – diese Texte sind weit entfernt von jenen heiteren aus der sommerlichen Pagerie. Obgleich das Titelwort »Irrstern« nur einmal in den Texten erscheint, liegt es allen zu Grunde, weil alle auf diesem Irrstern entstanden sind, und in seines ständigen Gedenken. »[. . .] es wird ein schlimmes Ende nehmen und bald« schließt einer, doch so eindeutig wie hier im verkürzenden Zitat ist auch dieser Text nicht. Vereindeutigungsversuche kommen dieser Prosa nicht bei. Denn sie bildet auch die Schizophrenie unserer alltäglichen Existenz ab, wie sie sich aus unserem selektiven Wahrnehmungsvermögen innerhalb einer zerfallenden und gleichzeitig komplexen und unüberschaubaren Welt aufschließen, ohne doch restlos erschlossen werden zu können. Noch in dem Prosa-Band *Schwingrasen* von 1991 ging Sarah Kirsch auf dieser Spur weiter, nahm dort freilich auch Texte auf, die sichtlich unverhüllte Erinnerungen waren, oder Aufzeichnungen aus dem Alltag. Solch autobiographisches Schreiben hat Sarah Kirsch in den beiden Bänden *Spreu* (ebenfalls 1991) und *Das simple Leben* von 1994 recht offen betrieben, eine ungewöhnliche Wendung in ihrem Werk: Erstmals stehen fast unverschlüsselte Berichte in ihrem Werk, gar in Tagebuchform, aber das so offene Mitgeteilte wird in bisweilen schnoddriger Sprache niedrig gehängt, ins *Allerlei-Rauh* von 1988, worin Sarah Kirsch eben jenen Sommer poetisch noch einmal beschwor, den Christa Wolf in ihrem *Sommerstück* nur wenig verhüllt nacherzählt hat: ein letzter langer Besuch bei der Freundin und den alten Freunden in Mecklenburg, in der DDR, die es nun nicht mehr gibt.

11

Bibliography

MERERID HOPWOOD

CONTENTS

1.   **Primary Literature**
1.a   Anthologies of poems
1.b   Anthologies of prose texts
1.c   Works for children
1.d   Illustrations and illustrated editions
1.e   Works edited/prefaced by Sarah Kirsch
1.f   Translations of Sarah Kirsch's work
1.g   Works translated by Sarah Kirsch
1.h   Essays, interviews, open letters and articles
1.i   Individual poems and texts
1.j   Radio plays, films, records and cassettes

Works are listed chronologically in each section apart from the sections **Works edited/prefaced by Sarah Kirsch**, and **Works translated by Sarah Kirsch**, where entries appear in alphabetical order according to the author's surname.

2.   **Secondary Literature**
Articles are listed alphabetically according to author's surname; a review is indicated by [R], and where a work is written by a collective it appears under its title.

1.   Primary Literature

1.a   Anthologies of poems

1. *Landaufenthalt. Gedichte* (Berlin, Weimar, Aufbau, 1967) [Lizenzausgabe: Ebenhausen bei München, Langewiesche-Brandt, 1969].
2. *Gedichte* (Leipzig, Reclam, 1967) [Lizenzausgabe: Ebenhausen bei München, Langewiesche-Brandt, 1969].
3. *Zaubersprüche* (Berlin, Weimar, Aufbau, 1973) [Lizenzausgabe: Ebenhausen bei München, Langewiesche-Brandt, 1974; illustrated by Dieter Goltsched, 1977].
4. *Es war dieser merkwürdige Sommer. Gedichte* (Berlin, Claassen, 1974).
5. *Rückenwind. Gedichte* (Berlin, Weimar, Aufbau, 1976) [Lizenzausgabe: Ebenhausen bei München, Langewiesche-Brandt, 1977].
6. *Musik auf dem Wassser. Gedichte*, an anthology from *Landaufenthalt, Zaubersprüche, Rückenwind* (Leipzig, Reclam, 1977) [2nd expanded edition, edited by Elke Erb, Lepizig, Reclam, 1989].
7. *Sommergedichte: Poetische Wandzeitung* (Ebenhausen bei München, Langewiesche-Brandt, 1978).
8. *Wintergedichte: Poetische Wandzeitung* (Ebenhausen bei München, Langewiesche-Brandt, 1978).
9. *Katzenkopfpflaster. Gedichte*, an anthology from *Landaufenthalt, Zaubersprüche, Rückenwind* (Munich, Deutscher Taschenbuch Verlag, 1978).
10. *Drachensteigen. Gedichte* (Ebenhausen bei München, Langewiesche-Brandt, 1979).
11. *Erdreich* (Stuttgart, Deutsche Verlags-Anstalt, 1982) [Blindendruck der Deutschen Blindenstudienanstalt Marburg, 1982 = Lizenz der Deutschen Verlags-Anstalt, Stuttgart].
12. *Der Winter: Gedichte* (Hauzenberg, Ed. Pongratz, 1983).
13. *Katzenleben* (Stuttgart, Deutsche Verlags-Anstalt, 1984).
14. *Landwege: Eine Auswahl 1980–85*, with afterword by Günter Kunert (Stuttgart, Deutsche Verlags-Anstalt, 1985).
15. *Hundert Gedichte* [an anthology from *Landaufenthalt, Zaubersprüche, Rückenwind, Drachensteigen*, and with a conversation between Hans Ester, Dick van Stekelenburg and Sarah Kirsch] (Ebenhausen bei München, Langewiesche-Brandt, 1985).
16. *Schneewärme. Gedichte* (Stuttgart, Deutsche Verlags-Anstalt, 1989).
17. *Die Flut: Auswahl von Gerhard Wolf* (Berlin, Weimar, Aufbau, 1989).
18. *Erlkönigs Tochter* (Stuttgart, Deutsche Verlags-Anstalt, 1992).
19. *Eisland. Zwölf Gedichte* (Warmbronn, Keicher, 1992).
20. *Bodenlos. Gedichte* (Stuttgart, Deutsche Verlags-Anstalt, 1996).

1.b   Anthologies of prose texts

1. *Die Pantherfrau: Fünf unfrisierte Erzählungen aus dem Kassetten-Recorder* (Berlin, Weimar, Aufbau, 1973) [West German edition: Ebenhausen bei München, Langewiesche-Brandt, 1975; paperback edition: Reinbek bei Hamburg, Rowohlt, 1978].

2. *Die ungeheuren bergehohen Wellen auf See. Erzählungen* (Berlin, Eulenspiegel, 1973) [expanded new edition with afterword by Jens Jessen: Zurich, Manesse, 1987].

3. 'Blitz aus heiterm Himmel', in Edith Anderson (ed.), *Blitz aus heiterm Himmel. Anthologie* (Rostock, Hinstorff, 1975); also in Sarah Kirsch, Irmtraud Morgner and Christa Wolf, *Geschlechtertausch* (Darmstadt, Neuwied, Luchterhand, 1980), 25–63.

4. *La Pagerie* (Stuttgart, Deutsche Verlags-Anstalt, 1980) [paperback edition, with an essay by Marcel Reich-Ranicki: Munich, Deutscher Taschenbuch Verlag, 1984].

5. *Irrstern. Prosa* (Stuttgart, Deutsche Verlags-Anstalt, 1986).

6. *Allerlei-Rauh. Eine Chronik* (Stuttgart, Deutsche Verlags-Anstalt, 1988).

7. *Schwingrasen. Prosa* (Stuttgart, Deutsche Verlags-Anstalt, 1991).

8. *Das simple Leben* (Stuttgart, Deutsche Verlags-Anstalt, 1994).

1.c   Works for children

1. *See, Die betrunkene Sonne, Der Stärkste,* with Rainer Kirsch (Berlin-Oberschöneweide, Staatliches Rundfunkkomitee, 1963) [new edition: Leipzig, Schulze, 1966].

2. *Hänsel und Gretel: Eine illustrierte Geschichte für kleine und große Leute nach der gleichnamigen Märchenoper von Adeleheid Wette und Engelbert Humperdink* (Leipzig, Frankfurt am Main, London, New York, Peters, 1972) [new edition with record: Leipzig, Peters, 1975].

3. *Zwischen Herbst und Winter: Kinderbuch,* with Ingrid Schuppau (Berlin, Kinderbuchverlag, 1975).

4. 'Das Lied von der Heerfahrt Igors', in *Sagen und Epen der Welt, neu erzählt* (Berlin, Kinderbuchverlag, 1977).

5. *Die betrunkene Sonne. Für Sprecher und Orchester: Ein Melodram für Kinder,* text by Sarah Kirsch, music by Tilo Medek (Leipzig, Peters, 1975) [bilingual edition, English version by Sandra Chappell: Frankfurt am Main, Hansen, 1978].

6. *Hans mein Igel: Nach den Kinder- und Hausmärchen der Gebrüder Grimm,* illustrated by Paula Schmidt (Cologne, Middelhauve, 1980) [also: Frankfurt am Main, Olten, Vienna, Büchergilde Gutenberg, 1982].

1.d Illustrations and illustrated editions

1. *Gespräch mit dem Saurier. Gedichte*, with Rainer Kirsch, colour illustrations by Ronald Paris (Berlin, Neues Leben, 1965).
2. *Ein Sommerregen*, with Kota Taniuchi (Hamburg, Wittig, 1978).
3. *Wind*, with Kota Taniuchi (Hamburg, Wittig, 1979).
4. *Schatten*, with Kota Taniuchi (Hamburg, Wittig, 1979).
5. *Zwischen Herbst und Winter*, with Kurt Mühlenhaupt (Cologne, Middelhauve, 1983) [=Middelhauve-Bilderbuch] [Lizenzausgabe: Zurich, Ex Libris, 1984].
6. *Galoschen: Immerwährender Kalender* (Bremen, Neue Bremer Presse, 1987).
7. *Luft und Wasser*, illustrated by Ingo Kühl (Göttingen, Steidl, 1988) [two numbered editions also appeared: *I–XXV*, drawings by Sarah Kirsch and original work by Ingo Kühl, signed by both artists; and *1–25*, signed by both artists].
8. *Tiger im Regen*, with Hyun-Sook Song (Ravensburg, Ravensburger Buchverlag, 1990).
9. *Spreu* (Göttingen, Steidl, 1991).
10. *Wasserbilder: Ein gemischtes Bündel* (Steidl, Göttingen, 1993).
11. *Ich Crusoe: sechzig Gedichte*, illustrated by Sarah Kirsch [foreword by Joachim Kaiser, afterword by Karin von Maur on the occasion of the author's 60th birthday, 16 April 1995] (Stuttgart, Deutsche Verlags-Anstalt, Ebenhausen bei München, Langewiesche-Brandt, 1995).

1.e Works edited/prefaced by Sarah Kirsch

1. Czechowski, Heinz, *Ich und die Folgen*, chosen and edited by Sarah Kirsch and Karin Kiwus in collaboration with the author (Reinbek bei Hamburg, Rowohlt 1987).
2. *Annette von Droste-Hülshoff*, selected by Sarah Kirsch (Cologne, Kiepenheuer & Witsch, 1986).
3. Erb, Elke, *Trost. Gedichte und Prosa*, selected by Sarah Kirsch (Stuttgart, Deutsche Verlags-Anstalt, 1982).
4. Gruša, Jiri, *Der Babylonwald. Gedichte 1988*, afterword by Sarah Kirsch (Stuttgart, Deutsche Verlags-Anstalt, 1991).
5. Neumann, Margarete, *Am Abend vor der Heimreise*, afterword by Sarah Kirsch (Berlin, Weimar, Aufbau, 1974).
6. Schubert, Helga, *Lauter Leben. Geschichten*, afterword by Sarah Kirsch (Berlin, Weimar, Aufbau, 1975).
7. Wegner, Bettina, *Wenn meine Lieder nicht mehr stimmen*, with a preface by Sarah Kirsch (Reinbek bei Hamburg, Rowohlt 1979).

1.f   Translations of Sarah Kirsch's work

1. 'Die Luft riecht schon nach Schnee', 'Das Grundstück', translated by David and Rene Gill, *Dimension*, Special Issue (1973), 132–5.
2. *Formule magiche. Con teste tedesco a fronte*, [*Zaubersprüche*] introduced and translated by Italo Alighero Chiusano (Milan, Rosconi, 1979).
3. 'Seit er fort ist. Landpost', 'Ich wollte meinen König töten', translated by Stewart Florsheim, *Dimension*, 12 (1979), 344–7.
4. 'Zwischenlandung', 'Anziehung', 'Das Fenster', 'Schwarze Bohnen', 'Bei den weissen Stiefmütterchen', 'Ich', 'In der Sonne deines Sterbemonats', 'Meine Worte gehorchen mir nicht', 'Raubvogel', translated by Almut McAuley, *Mundus Artium*, 11 (1979), 2 and 24–31.
5. Zwei Gedichte. – 'Der Milan'. 'Viel' / Two Poems – 'The Red Kite'. 'Much', translated by Helmbrecht Breinig and Kevin Power, *Dimension*, 14 (1981), 280–1.
6. *Conjurations*, selected and translated by Wayne Kvam (Ohio, London, Ohio University Press, 1985).
7. *Erdreich = Terre*, Sarah Kirsch Poèmes, translated and presented by Jean-Paul Barbe (éd. Bilingue Saint Florent-des Bois et De Bleu, 1988).
8. *The Brontës Hat*, translated by Wendy Mulford and Anthony Vivis (Cambridge, Street Editions, 1991).
9. *Winter Music*, selected poems by Sarah Kirsch, translated by Margitt Lehbert (London, Anvil Press, 1994).

1.g   Works translated by Sarah Kirsch

1. Achmatowa, Anna, *Ein niedagewesener Herbst, Gedichte Russisch-Deutsch*, edited by Edel Mirowa Florin, translated from the Russian original by Sarah Kirsch and Rainer Kirsch (Berlin, Kultur und Fortschritt, 1967).
2. Baczynski, Krzyszof Kamil, 'Die Erde die Feuersäule', translated from the Polish original by Sarah Kirsch, *Neue Deutsche Literatur*, 22 No. 7 (1974), 40–41.
3. Grieg, Nordahl, 'Preiselbeermarmelade', translated from the Norwegian original by Sarah Kirsch, *Poesie*, 5 No. 4 (1977), 12–13.
4. Kincaid, Jamaica, *At the bottom of the river/Am Grunde des Flusses*, translated from the American original by Sarah Kirsch and Moritz Kirsch (Stuttgart, Deutsche Verlags-Anstalt, 1986).
5. Marcinkevicius, Justinas, 'Des Vogels Flug', 'Unterm hohen Stern', 'Der Blick', translated from the Russian original by Sarah Kirsch, *Neue Deutsche Literatur*, 23 No. 7 (1975), 56–8.
6. Matwejewa, Novella, *Gedichte*, chosen by Fritz Mierau; German versions by Sarah Kirsch and Eckhard Ulrich, illustrated by Peter Nagengast (Berlin, Neues Leben, 1968) [=Poesiealbum, 6].

7. Osiecka, Agnieszka, *Appetit auf Frühkirschen. Spiel für zwei Personen*, lyrics translated by Sarah Kirsch, music by Tilo Medek (Berlin, Henschel, 1971).

8. Simonow, Konstantin, 'Vietnam', 'Winter Siebzig', 'Für Genossin To-Hui', translated from the Russian original by Sarah Kirsch, *Sinn und Form*, 25 (1973), 5–6.

9. Sjoegren, Lennart, *Gedichte*, German versions of the Swedish originals by Sarah Kirsch and Erich Schwandt, *Akzente*, 31 (1984), 55–66.

10. Wassiljewa, Larissa, *Gedichte*, chosen by Herbert Krempien, translated by Sarah Kirsch and Ilse Krätzig, illustrated by Wsewolod Brodski (Berlin, Neues Leben, 1971) [=Poesiealbum, 47].

1.h Essays, interviews, open letters and articles

1. *Berlin-Sonnenseite. Deutschlandtreffen der Jugend in der Hauptstadt der DDR. Bildreportage*, with Thomas Billhardt and Rainer Kirsch (Berlin, Neues Leben, 1964).

2. *Vietnam in dieser Stunde: Dokumentation*, with Werner Bräunig, F. Cremer, Peter Gosse and Rainer Kirsch (Halle, Mitteldeutscher, 1968) [Lizenzausgabe: Zurich, Limmat, 1969].

3. 'Gedichte einer Töpferin: Zum lyrischen Werk von Christiana Grosz', *Neue Deutsche Literatur*, 25 No. 2 (1977), 101.

4. *Erklärungen einiger Dinge. Gespräch mit Schülern*, with contributions by Urs Widmer and Elke Erb (Ebenhausen bei München, Langewiesche-Brandt, 1978) [paperback edition: Reinbek bei Hamburg, Rowohlt, 1981; also as: 'Erklärung einiger Dinge', from the volume of the same title, edited by Erhard Schnepf, *Deutscher Germanistenverband*, 26 No. 2 (1979), 37–40].

5. 'Über Nicolas Born', *Deutsche Akademie für Sprache und Dichtung* (1979), 2, 112–13.

6. Interview: 'Von der volkseigenen Idylle ins freie Land der Wölfe: Ein Gespräch mit Sarah Kirsch', questions asked by Klaus Wagenbach, *Freibeuter*, 2 (1979), 85–93.

7. 'Vier deutsche Schriftsteller, die in Berlin leben [Thomas Brasch, Günter Grass, Sarah Kirsch und Peter Schneider] rufen zum Frieden auf', in Ingrid Krüger (ed.), *Mut zur Angst, Schriftsteller für den Frieden* (Darmstadt, Neuwied, Luchterhand, 1982), 18–19 [open letter to Helmut Schmidt, 17 April 1980].

8. Interview: 'Some Comments and a Conversation', Peter Graves and Sarah Kirsch, *German Life and Letters*, 44 (1990–91), 271–80.

9. Interview: '"Ich bin sehr hart und sehr streng mit Menschen": Ein Gespräch mit Sarah Kirsch', Antje Peters-Hirt and Sarah Kirsch, *Euterpe*, 9 (1991), 38–45.

1.i   Individual poems and texts

1. 'Schöner Morgen'. Hierzulande', *Auftakt*, 63 (1963), 37–8.
2. 'Mond vor meinem Fenster', 'Bekanntschaft', *Neue Deutsche Literatur*, 6 No. 4 (1963), 145–6.
3. 'Zehn Gedichte mit einer Illustration', *Sonnenpferde und Astronauten: Gedichte junger Menschen* (Jena, Saale, 1964), 49–58.
4. 'Kleine Adresse', 'Eichelhähe', 'Der Himmel schuppt sich', *Konkret*, 5 (1965), 32.
5. 'Mond vor meinem Fenster', *Nachricht von den Liebenden: Gedichte und Photos* (Berlin, Weimar, Aufbau, 1965), 30–1.
6. 'Sanft kommt der Herbst', *Nachricht von den Liebenden: Gedichte und Photos* (Berlin, Weimar, Aufbau, 1965), 41–2.
7. 'Schöner Morgen', *Nachricht von den Liebenden: Gedichte und Photos* (Berlin, Weimar, Aufbau,1965), 52.
8. 'April, letzte Drittel', *Nachricht von den Liebenden: Gedichte und Photos* (Berlin, Weimar, Aufbau, 1965) 61–2.
9. 'Acht Neue Gedichte', *Neue Deutsche Literatur*, 13 No. 2 (1965), 38–44.
10. 'Vier Gedichte', *Neue Deutsche Literatur*, 13 No. 10 (1965), 63–5.
11. '12.9.65' [day on which the death of the poet Johannes Bobrowski was announced], 'Ich bin in der Sonne deines Sterbemonats', 'Ausflug', *Kürbiskern*, 1 (1966), 91–2.
12. 'Legende über Lilja', *Kürbiskern*, 2 (1966), 120–1.
13. 'Hirtenlied', *Neue Deutsche Literatur*, 17 No. 7/8 (1966), 108.
14. 'Bäume lesen', *An alle Berlin* (1967), 91–2.
15. 'Gedichte' [seven poems], *Kübiskern*, 1 (1967), 60–5.
16. 'Der Schnee liegt schwarz in meiner Stadt', *Luchterhands Loseblattlyrik*, 3 (1967), 5.
17. 'Bäume lesen', 'Chagall in Witebsk', *Neue Texte. Almanach für deutsche Literatur. Herbst 1967*, vol. 6 (Berlin, Weimar, Aufbau, 1967), 5–6.
18. 'Bevor die Sonne aufgeht', 'Augenblick', 'Eines Tages' [three poems for Vietnam], *Neue Texte. Almanach für deutsche Literatur. Herbst 1967*, vol. 6 (Berlin, Weimar, Aufbau,1967), 12–13.
19. 'Chagall in Witebsk', *Lyrik aus dieser Zeit*, 4 (1967–68), 9.
20. 'Ich lag auf dem Badestag', *Lyrik aus dieser Zeit*, 4 (1967–68), 37.
21. 'Bilder', *Luchterhands Loseblattlyrik*, 11 (1968), 4.
22. 'Gedichte' [nine poems], *Neue Texte* (Berlin, 1968), 36–43.
23. 'Schwarze Bohnen', *Tintenfisch*, 1 (1968), 32.
24. 'Und dann gingen wir noch', *Luchterhands Loseblattlyrik*, 16 (1969), 5.
25. 'Der Schnee liegt schwarz', *Merian*, 23 No. 1 (1971), 94.
26. 'Muskelkater', in Rainer Kirsch (ed.), *Olympische Spiele* (Berlin, Aufbau, 1972), 35.
27. 'Angeln', in Rainer Kirsch (ed.), *Olympische Spiele* (Berlin, Aufbau, 1972), 54–5.

28. 'Die Luft riecht schon nach Schnee', 'Das Grundstück', German and English translated by David and Rene Gill, *Dimension*, Special Issue (1973), 132–5.

29. 'Märchen im Schrank', 'Tilia Spec', *Neue Deutsche Literatur*, 21 No. 6, (1973), 28–9.

30. 'Eines Tages', 'Petzkow Kreis Werder', *Text + Kritik*, 9/9a (1973), 69.

31. 'Die ungeheuren bergehohen Wellen auf See', in Stefan Heym (ed.), *Auskunft: neue Prosa aus der DDR* (Munich, AutorenEdition, 1974), 172–7.

32. 'Schule der guten Laune', *DDR-Reportagen* (Leipzig, 1974), 237–45.

33. 'Schwarze Bohnen', *Dokumente*, 30 (1974), 73.

34. 'Brief an H. A. P. Grieshaber', in H. A. P. Grieshaber (ed.), *Der Engel der Geschichte* (Stuttgart, Manus Presse,1974),10.

35. 'Der Droste würde ich gern Wasser reichen', 'Ich', *Ensemble*, 5 (1974), 82–3.

36. 'Zwillinge', *Kürbiskern*, 2 (1974), 53–9.

37. 'Der Merposvogel', 'Wiepersdorf Viertel Abend', *Literaturmagazin*, No. 2 (1974), 155–6.

38. 'Warum die wilde sich bäumende Musik am Ohrid-See plötzlich schweigt', in Rainer Kirsch (ed.), *Das letzte Mahl mit der Geliebten* (Berlin, Eulenspiegel, 1975), 72–4.

39. 'Der Schmied von Kosewack' [prose text], *Merkur*, 29 (1975), 145–51.

40. 'Rückenwind', 'Warum die wilde sich bäumende Musik am Ohrid-See plötzlich schweigt', 'Der Meropsvogel', 'Wenn es nach mir ginge, ich sässe den Tag', *Neue Deutsche Literatur*, 23 No. 12 (1975), 104–6.

41. 'Der Milan' [six poems], *Manuskripte*, 15 No. 51 (1975–76), 36–7.

42. 'Im Juni', 'Rückenwind', *Akzente*, 23 (1976), 291–2.

43. 'Nach Shanghai und zurück. Aus dem Leben der Genossin Genia Nobel' [prose text], in Alice Uskorzeit (ed.), *Bekanntschaften* (Berlin, Weimar, 1976), 5–24.

44. 'Vier Gedichte', *Berliner Schriftsteller erzählen* (Berlin, 1976), 246–8.

45. 'Tilia Cordata', 'Die Luft riecht schon nach Schnee', 'Im Juni', *Litfass*, 4 (1976), 17–18.

46. 'Doppel-Landschaften' [twelve poems], *Neue Deutsche Literatur*, 24 No. 9 (1976), 100–3.

47. 'Der Schmied von Kosewalk', in Joachim Walter and Manfred Wolter (eds.), *Die Rettung des Saragossameeres* (Berlin, Buchverlag der Morgen, 1976), 302–10.

48. 'Neun Gedichte', *Sinn und Form*, 28 (1976), 583–8.

49. 'Fünf Gedichte', *Orte*, 3 (1976–7), 12, 28–31.

50. 'Spiegelungen', *Merkur*, 31 (1977), 163–4.

51. 'Im Sommer', *Tintenfisch*, 12 (1977), 63.

52. 'Im Juni', in Ulrich Berkes (ed.), *Vor meinen Augen, hinter sieben Bergen* (Berlin, Aufbau, 1977), 50.

53. 'Markttag', in Ulrich Berkes (ed.), *Vor meinen Augen, hinter sieben Bergen* (Berlin, Aufbau, 1977), 142.
54. 'Acht Gedichte', *Hermannstraße*, 14 No. 1 (1978), 92–9.
55. 'Post', *Nürnberger Blätter für Literatur*, 4 (1978), 11.
56. 'The last of November', *Nürnberger Blätter für Literatur*, 4 (1978), 13.
57. 'Oder die Fahnen am Markusplatz', *Nürnberger Blätter für Literatur*, 4 (1978), 18.
58. 'Der Rest des Fadens', *Nürnberger Blätter für Literatur*, 4 (1978), 21.
59. 'Unsere Bäume', *Nürnberger Blätter für Literatur*, 4 (1978), 49.
60. 'Steck dir Dein', *Nürnberger Blätter für Literatur*, 4 (1978), 55.
61. 'Der Kam', *Tintenfisch*, 14 (1978), 8.
62. 'Das weltbürgerliche Kamel', in Gregor Laschen (ed.), *Der zerstückte Traum: Für Erich Arendt* (Berlin, Darmstadt, Agora, 1978), 172.
63. 'Italienische Amseln', *Claassen Jahrbuch der Lyrik*, 1 (1979), 43.
64. 'Getrennt', *Claassen Jahrbuch der Lyrik*, 1 (1979), 63.
65. 'Seit er fort ist', 'Landpost', 'Ich wollte meinen König töten', German and English, translated by Stewart Florsheim, *Dimension*, 12 (1979), 344–7.
66. 'Im Glashaus des Schneekönigs', in Ingeborg Drewitz (ed.), *Hoffnungsgeschichten*, (Gütersloh, Gütersloher Verlagshaus Mohn, 1979), 164.
67. 'Sechs Gedichte', *Bunker*, 2 (1979), 77–80.
68. 'Zwischenlandung', 'Anziehung', 'Das Fenster', 'Schwarze Bohnen', 'Bei den weissen Stiefmütterchen', 'Ich in der Sonne deines Sterbemonats', 'Meine Worten gehorchen mir nicht', 'Raubvogel', German and English, translated by Almut McAuley, *Mundus Artium*, 11 (1979), 24–31.
69. 'Early in the morning' [for H. A. P. Grieshaber], *Schnittlein*, (Düsseldorf, 1979), 33.
70. 'Sieben Gedichte', *Petrarca-Preis 1975–9*, (Munich, 1980), 135–8.
71. 'Der Meropsvogel', 'Ende Mai', *Petrarca-Preis 1975–9* (Munich, 1980), 215–16.
72. 'Wechselbalg', 'Beginn der Zerstörung', *Akzente*, 28 (1981), 554–5.
73. 'Der Milan', 'Viel' / 'The Red Kite', 'Much', German and English, translated by Helmbrecht Breinig and Kevin Power, *Dimension*, 14 (1981), 280–1.
74. 'Der Eislauf', *Manuskripte*, 21 (1981), 16.
75. 'Don Juan kommt am Vormittag', *Westermanns Monatshefte*, 2 (1981), 27.
76. 'The Last of November', *Zwanzig Jahre Berliner Handpresse (1961–81)* (Berlin, Berliner Handpresse, 1981), 36.
77. 'Die ungeheuren bergehohen Wellen auf See' / 'The Enormous Mountainous Waves at Sea', German and English, translated by Carol Bedwell, *Dimension*, 15 (1982), 466–73.

78. 'Eichen und Rosen', *Jahrbuch Deutsche Akademie für Sprache und Dichtung*, 1 (1982), 66.
79. 'Vier Gedichte', *Poesie*, 10 No 1, (1982), 1–4.
80. 'Sanfter Schrecken', 'Gasthaus', 'Musikstunde', *Litfass*, 7 (1982–83), 28 and 82–4.
81. 'Der Winter' [21 poems], *Akzente*, 30 (1983), 3–15.
82. 'Falscher Hase', *Pfaffenweiler Literatur*, 18 (1983), 33.
83. 'Reisezehrung' [cycle of poems], *Tintenfisch*, 22 (1983), 29–32.
84. 'Sechs Gedichte', *L'80*, 29 (1984), 77–80.
85. 'Der Rest des Fadens', 'Dann werden wir kein Feuer brauchen', J. Monika Walther (ed.), *Lesebuch Zukunft* (Münster, Tende, 1984), 35–6.
86. 'Spielraum', 'Der süße Brei', 'Glatteis' [prose texts], *Euterpe*, 3 (1985), 23.
87. 'Montgolfiere', Kristina Pfoser-Schewig (ed.), *Für Ernst Jandl. Texte zum 60. Geburtstag. Werkgeschichte* (Vienna, Forschungs- und Dokumentationsstelle für Neuere Österreichische Literatur, 1985), 25.
88. 'Zwillinge' [from: *Die Pantherfrau*], in Ingrid Krueger (ed.), *Kommen wir zur Tagesordnung: Literarische Reportagen aus der DDR* (Darmstadt, Neuwied, Luchterhand, 1985), 112–20.
89. 'Vier Gedichte', *Luchterhand-Jahrbuch der Lyrik* (1985), 95–6.
90. 'Schäferstunde' [three prose texts], *Manuskripte*, 25 No. 89/90 (1985), 130–1.
91. 'Keiner hat mich verlassen', *Poesie*, 13 No. 4 (1985), 25.
92. 'Zehn Jahre Litfass. Eine Auswahl. Beiträge von Sarah Kirsch usw', *Litfass*, 10 (1986), 40, 1–63.
93. 'Mainacht', *Luchterhand-Jahrbuch der Lyrik* (1986), 17.
94. 'Schwarzer Spiegel', *Luchterhand-Jahrbuch der Lyrik* (1986), 120–2.
95. 'Ort und Stelle', 'Eichbäume', *Passauer Pegasus*, 4 No. 9 (1986), 48.
96. 'Entfernung', *Spektrum*, 29 No. 115 (1986–87), 13.
97. *Silent Rooms*, text by Sascha Anderson, Sarah Kirsch, Gerhard Falkner, Frank-Wolfgang Matthias, Bert Papenfuß-Gorek, Michael Rom, Kiev Stingl, Peter Waterhouse, Ernest Wichner. Illustrated by Wolfram Adalbert Scheffler, *et al.* (Berlin, Edition Malerbücher, 1987), 1.
98. 'Die Flügel des Fensters', 'Die Flut', *Träume: Literaturalmanach 1987* (Salzburg, Vienna, 1987), 77–8.
99. 'Chiropteren', *Luchterhand-Jahrbuch der Lyrik* (1987–88), 39.
100. 'Luft und Wasser', *Luchterhand-Jahrbuch der Lyrik* (1987–88), 60.
101. 'Freyas Katzen', *Luchterhand-Jahrbuch der Lyrik* (1987–88), 79.
102. 'Erdreich', 'Erdrauch', *Euterpe*, 6 (1988), 48–49.
103. 'Im Winter', 'Der Frühling', 'Verstohlen geht wieder der Mond auf', *Luchterhand-Jahrbuch der Lyrik* (1988–89), 68–70.
104. 'Krähengeschwätz', *Luchterhand-Jahrbuch der Lyrik* (1988–89), 91.
105. 'Vier Gedichte', *Euterpe*, 7 (1989), 31–4.

106. 'Keiner hat mich . . . ', in Helga Pankoke and Wolfgang Trampe (eds.), *Selbstbildnis zwei Uhr nachts* (Berlin, Weimar, Aufbau, 1989), 97.
107. 'Besinnung', in Helga Pankoke and Wolfgang Trampe (eds.), *Selbstbildnis zwei Uhr nachts* (Berlin, Weimar, Aufbau, 1989), 195.
108. 'Keiner hat mich . . . ' [facsimile of handwriting], *Text + Kritik*, 101 (1989), 3.
109. 'Nachgetragene Gedichte' [eight poems], *Text + Kritik*, 101 (1989), 10–12.
110. 'Schwarzer Spiegel', *Text + Kritik*, 101 (1989), 29–31.
111. 'Das Nebelhorn', 'Grund und Boden' [prose texts], *Text + Kritik*, 101 (1989), 68.
112. 'Allerlei-Rauh' [two pages from the *Allerlei-Rauh* manuscript], *Text + Kritik*, 101 (1989), 74–5.
113. 'Vier Gedichte', *Euterpe*, 8 (1990), 38–9.
114. 'Kleine Betrachtung am Morgen des 17. Novembers', in Michael Naumann (ed.), *Die Geschichte ist offen. DDR 1990: Hoffnung auf eine neue Republik. Schriftsteller aus der DDR über die Zukunftschancen ihres Landes* (Reinbek bei Hamburg, Rowohlt, 1990), 79–81.
115. 'Rede bei der Aufnahme als Mitglied in die Deutsche Akademie für Sprache und Dichtung', *Jahrbuch Deutsche Akademie für Sprache und Dichtung* (1990), 135–7.
116. 'Nächtlicherweile' [for Heiner Müller], *Jahrbuch zur Literatur in der DDR*, 7 (1990), 9.
117. 'Wintergarten I', 'Wintergarten II', *Literatur-Bote*, 5 (1990), 17 and 21.
118. 'Pfeffer und Salz' [prose texts], *Manuskripte*, 30 No. 110 (1990), 87.
119. 'Erdenliebe', *Neue Rundschau*, 101 No. 1 (1990), 38.
120. 'Was ich in Norwegen lernte', 'Watt', 'Stimmen', *Luchterhand-Jahrbuch der Lyrik* (1990–91), 109–10.
121. 'Sechs Gedichte', *Manuskripte*, 31 No. 112 (1991), 21.
122. 'Mauer', *Jahrbuch der Lyrik*, 8 (1992), 85–6.
123. 'Nothelfer im Gebirge', 'Erdenliebe', *Jahrbuch der Lyrik*, 8 (1992), 88–9.
124. 'Crusoe', *Litfass*, 16 (1992), 56, 29.
125. '"O Falada da du hangest": Rede zur Verleihung der Ehrengabe der Heine-Gesellschaft 1992', *Heine-Jahrbuch*, 32 (1993), 171.
126. 'Gefieder', in Thomas Rietzschel (ed.), *Über Deutschland. Schriftsteller geben Auskunft* (Leipzig, Reclam, 1993), 1–2.
127. 'Arbeit', in Thomas Rietzschel (ed.), *Über Deutschland. Schriftsteller geben Auskunft* (Leipzig, Reclam, 1993), 15.
128. 'Gedichte', *Akzente*, 41 (1994), 92–5.

1.j Radio plays, films, records and cassettes
1. *Die betrunkene Sonne*, for *GDR Radio*, 1962.
2. *Briefe an eine Freundin*, for ZDF, 1988.
3. *Die betrunkene Sonne. Ein Melodram für Kinder*, for *Deutsche Schallplatten* (Berlin, 1972) [=NOVA 885019], and for *Deutsche Grammophon* (Berlin, 1981) [=DG Junior 2546054 and DG3346054, cassette].
4. *Hänsel und Gretel* (record), (Leipzig, Peters) 1975.
5. *Sarah Kirsch liest Gedichte* (record), (Ebenhausen bei München, Langewiesche-Brandt, 1978) [=0647014].
6. *Es riecht nach Tang, Salz und Wahrheit – Sarah Kirsch in Wales*, directed by Claus Spahn and Karl Heinz Bahls for *Westdeutscher Rundfunk*, 13 July 1994.

2. Secondary Literature

1. Adam, Christine, 'Gedichte aus *Eisland*: Sarah Kirsch empfing in Freiburg den Gedok-Literaturpreis', *Badische Zeitung*, 25 May 1993.
2. Amster, Charlotte E., '"Merkwürdiges Beispiel weiblicher Entschlossenheit" – a woman's story – by Sarah Kirsch', in Margy Gerber (ed.), *Studies in GDR Culture and Society 2. Proceedings of the Seventh International Symposium on the German Democratic Republic* (Washington, University Press of Ameica, 1981), 243–50.
3. Arend, Angelika, 'The poetics of Sarah Kirsch: The task of remembering and historical consciousness', *Seminar*, 28 (1992), 89–91.
4. Arnold, Heinz Ludwig (ed.), *Sarah Kirsch, Text + Kritik*, 101 (1989).
5. Baron, Ulrich, 'Empört Euch, der Himmel ist blau: Sarah Kirschs *Das Simple Leben*', *Rheinischer Merkur*, 25 March 1994.
6. Baumgartner, Ekkehart, 'Die Republik ist in Gefahr: Drei deutsche Schriftsteller über Ausländerfeindlichkeit, die ehemalige DDR und Rechtsextremismus', *Süddeutsche Zeitung*, 2–4 October 1992.
7. Behn-Liebherz, Manfred, 'Sarah Kirsch', in Heinz Punkus (ed.), *Neue Literatur der Frauen. Deutschsprachige Autorinnen der Gegenwart* (Munich, Beck, 1980), 158–65.
8. Berendse, Gerrit-Jan, *Die sächsische Dichterschule: Lyrik in der DDR der 60er und 70er Jahre* (Frankfurt am Main, Bern, New York, Peter Lang, 1990).
9. Berke, Bernd, 'Die schlimmen Nachrichten dringen bis in den Elfenbeinturm', *Westfälische Rundschau*, 16 June 1994.
10. Beuchler, Klaus, 'Erlkönigs Tochter im Land der Trolle: Zeit- und Naturbilder von Sarah Kirsch', *Berliner Zeitung*, 30 September 1992.
11. Bienek, Horst, 'Liebe und Schnee', in *Frankfurter Anthologie*, 9 (Frankfurt am Main, Insel, 1985), 234–5 [on: 'Die Luft riecht schon nach Schnee'].

12. Bilen, Huelya, '"Der Meropsvogel" von Sarah Kirsch', in *Die Mauersegler*, (Aalborg, 1992), 69–72.

13. Bilke, Jeorg Bernhard, 'Die Lesereise der Sarah Kirsch: Bericht von einer Dichterlesung an der auch Bernd Jentzsch beteiligt war', *Der Literat*, 20 (1978), 10.

14. Bjorklund, Beth, '"Schwingrasen", Sarah Kirsch', *World Literature Today*, 66 (1992), 718.

15. Bondy, Barbara, 'Unbefangenheit der Trauer: Neue Gedichte von Sarah Kirsch' [R: *Erlkönigs Tochter*], *Süddeutsche Zeitung*, 30 September 92.

16. Bormann, Alexander von, '"Zu preisen ist nicht viel": Nüchterne Passion, opake Trauer, alarmierte Einfühlung – Gedichte von Sarah Kirsch' [R: *Erlkönigs Tochter*], *Frankfurter Rundschau*, 5 December 1992.

17. ——, '"Es wäxt nichts mehr": Sarah Kirschs Tagebuch *Das simple Leben*', *Frankfurter Rundschau*, 19 July 1994.

18. Braun, Michael, 'Erlkönigs Töchter: Neue Gedichte von Sarah Kirsch, Friederike Mayröcker, Karin Kiwus und Evelyn Schlag', *die tageszeitung*, 30 September 1992.

19. Brettschneider, Werner, 'Reiner Kunze und Gefährten: Zur Lyrik Reiner Kunzes, Uwe Greßmans, Sarah Kirschs', in W. Brettschneider (ed.), *Zwischen literarischer Autonomie und Staatsdienst: Die Literatur in der DDR* (Berlin, E. Schmidt, 1972), 227–34.

20. Buch, Hans Christoph, 'Die Stunde der Dichter', *Die Zeit*, 4 December 1992.

21. Butler, Michael, 'Der sanfte Mut der Melancholie: Zur Liebeslyrik Sarah Kirschs', *Text + Kritik*, 101 (1989), 52–60.

22. Cosentino, Christine, 'Die Lyrikerin Sarah Kirsch im Spiegel ihrer Bilder', *Neophilologus*, 63 (1979), 418–29.

23. ——, 'Privates und Politisches: Zur Frage des offenen Spielraums in der Lyrik Sarah Kirschs', *Germanic Notes*, 10 (1979), 17–20.

24. ——, 'Sarah Kirschs Dichtung in der DDR: Ein Rückblick', *German Studies Review*, 4 (1981), 105–16.

25. ——, 'Von "italienischen Amseln" und "provenzalischen Eulen": Sarah Kirschs westliche Dichtungen *Drachensteigen* und *La Pagerie*', in Margy Gerber (ed.), *Studies in GDR Culture and Society 2. Proceedings of the Seventh International Symposium on the German Democratic Republic* (Washington, University Press of America, 1981), 87–98.

26. ——, 'Literary correlation between Sarah Kirsch's poem "Der Rest des Fadens" and Elke Erbe's volume *Der Faden der Geduld*', *GDR Monitor*, 5 (1981), 52–6.

27. ——, 'Sarah Kirschs Lyrikband *Drachensteigen*: Eine Neuorientierung?', *Michigan Germanic Studies*, 9 (1983), 63–74.

28. ——, '"Ich gedenke nicht an Heimweh zu sterben": Überlegungen zu Sarah Kirschs Lyrikband _Erdreich_', in Ian Wallace (ed.), _The GDR in the 1980s_ (Dundee, University of Dundee Press, 1984), 121–33.

29. ——, '"Seßhafte Ambulanz": Zum Bild der Katze in Sarah Kirschs Lyrikband _Katzenleben_', _Germanic Notes_, 18 (1987), 7–11.

30. ——, '"Gegenwärtige Zeit die auch in Zukunft/Vergangenheit heißt wie meine": DDR-Reminiszenzen in Sarah Kirschs _Katzenleben_ und _Irrstern_', _Studies in GDR Culture_, 8 (Lanham, London, University Press of America, 1988), 141–54.

31. ——, _'Ein Spiegel mit mir darin': Sarah Kirschs Lyrik_ (Tübingen, Francke, 1990).

32. ——, 'Sarah Kirsch in Ost und West', in Axel Goodbody and Dennis Tate (eds.), _Geist und Macht: Writers and the State in the GDR_ (Amsterdam, Rodopi, 1992), 163–72.

33. Cott, Georg Oswald, '"Bockig salopp": Sarah Kirsch verbindet Aquarell und Prosa' [R: _Sic! natur_], _Deutsches Allgemeines Sonntagsblatt_, 4 December 1992.

34. Czechowski, Heinz, 'Zu Gast bei den Trollen', _Die Welt_, 29 September 1992.

35. ——, 'Das Wiedererscheinen Sarah Kirschs in der Menge', _Börsenblatt_, 6 December 1991.

36. Damm, Sigrid, 'bau ich dir vierblättrigen Klee', _Neue Deutsche Literatur_, 11 (1973), 121–6.

37. ——, 'Sarah Kirsch: _Rückenwind_', _Weimarer Beiträge_, 3 (1977), 131–41.

38. Demmer, Sybille, '"Schnee fällt uns / Mitten ins Herz hinein": Naturbildlichkeit und Liebeserlebnis in Sarah Kirsch's Gedicht "Die Luft riecht schon nach Schnee"', in Walter Hinck (ed.), _Gedichte und Interpretationen_, vol. 6 (Stuttgart, Reclam, 1982), 351–9.

39. Demmer, Justus, '"Aber meine Grundhaltung ist die Melancholie"', _General-Anzeiger_, 15–16 April 1995.

40. Detering, Heinrich, 'Ankunft auf dem Meeresgrund: _Erlkönigs Tochter_; Naturlyrik am Ende der Natur', _Frankfurter Allgemeine Zeitung_, 29 September 1992.

41. Dittberner, Hugo, 'Artistin zu eigenen Gnaden. Ein Essay über Sarah Kirsch', _Text + Kritik_, 101 (1989), 4–9.

42. Donahue, N. H., 'The poetics of Kirsch, Sarah – The task of remembering and historical consciousness', in Barbara Mabee (ed.), _German Studies Review_, 4 (1991), 673–4.

43. Dönselmann, Petra, '"Das Eis auf dem See hat Risse": Zu Sarah Kirschs Lyrik', _Spuren_, 1 (1978), 24–6.

44. Egyptien, Jürgen, 'Schweigesprache und Schreckwehpoem: Zum lyrischen Werk von Erika Burkart und Sarah Kirsch', in Dieter Breuer (ed.), _Deutsche Lyrik nach 1945_ (Frankfurt am Main, Suhrkamp, 1988), 321–53.

45. ——, '"Im Park des Hermaphroditen": Sarah Kirschs "Wiepersdorf-Zyklus" im Gedichtband *Rückenwind'*, *Text + Kritik*, 101 (1989), 61–7.

46. Eigler, Friederike, '"Verlorene Zeit, gewonnener Raum": Sarah Kirschs Abschied von der DDR in *Allerlei-Rauh'*, *Monatshefte*, 83 (1991), 176–89.

47. Endler, Adolf, 'Sarah Kirsch und ihre Kritiker', *Sinn und Form*, 27 (1975), 142–70.

48. ——, 'Randnotiz über die Engel Sarah Kirschs', *Text + Kritik*, 101 (1989), 32–40.

49. Engler, Jürgen, 'Zauberhafte Prosa: zu Sarah Kirschs *Spreu'* [R], *Neue Deutsche Literatur*, No. 39 (1991), 152–3.

50. ——, 'Glück im Unglück', *Neue Deutsche Literatur*, 41 No. 3 (1993), 483.

51. Erb, Elke, 'Nachwort', in Sarah Kirsch, *Musik auf dem Wasser* (Leipzig, Reclam, 1977), 83–95; also in Sarah Kirsch, *Erklärung einiger Dinge* (Ebenhausen bei München, Langewiesche-Brandt, 1978), 56–74.

52. Ester, Hans, 'Nieuwe poezie van Sarah Kirsch', *De Gids*, 146 (1983), 311–14.

53. ——, Stekelenburg, Dick van, 'Sarah Kirsch', in Gerd Labroisse and Ian Wallace (eds.), *DDR Schriftsteller sprechen in der Zeit: Eine Dokumentation* (Amsterdam, Rodopi, 1991), 69–79.

54. Fehn, Ann Clark, 'Authorial Voice in Sarah Kirsch's *Die Pantherfrau'*, in Walter F. W. Lohner and Martha Woodmansee (eds.), *Erkennen und Deuten: Essays zur Literatur und Literaturtheorie, Edgar Lohner in Memoriam* (Berlin, E. Schmidt, 1983), 335–46.

55. Figge, Susan G., '"Der Wunsch nach Welt": The Travel Motif in the Poetry of Sarah Kirsch', in Margy Gerber (ed.), *Studies in GDR Culture and Society, Proceedings of the 6th International Symposium on the German Democratic Republic* (Washington, University Press of America, 1981), 167–84.

56. Flood, John L. (ed.), *Ein Moment des erfahrenen Lebens. Zur Lyrik der DDR* (Amsterdam, Rodopi, 1987) [=*GDR Monitor* Special Series, 5].

57. Freudenstern, Christiane, 'Bibliografie', *Text + Kritik*, 101 (1989), 90–100.

58. Fritz, Walter Helmut, '"Ein gerüttelter Maß wahnsinniger Zuneigung". Sarah Kirschs Prosa', *Text + Kritik*, 101 (1989), 76–81.

59. Fritz, Walter Helmut, 'Spröde Intensität', *Frankfurter Hefte*, 38 No. 10 (1977), 74–8.

60. Frühwald, Wolfgang, 'Die Sanftheit der Sarah Kirsch', *Frankfurter Allgemeine Zeitung*, 7 August 1993.

61. ——, 'Die "Endlichkeit dieser Erde": Laudatio auf Sarah Kirsch (anläßlich der Verleihung des Literaturpreises der Konrad-Adenauer-Stiftung 1993)', *Sinn und Form*, 45 (1993), 673–8.

62. Fühmann, Franz, 'Vademecum für Leser von Zaubersprüchen', *Sinn und Form*, 27 (1975), 385–420.

63. Furtado, Maria Teresa Dias, 'Entrevista a Sarah Kirsch', *Runa* (1992), 267–71.

64. Gahse, Zsuzsanna, 'Rundflug', *Text + Kritik*, 101 (1989), 41–5.

65. Giesecke, Almut, 'Zum Leistungsvermögen einer Prosaform: Analysen zu "Der Schmied von Kosewalkg" von Sarah Kirsch und "Juninachmittag" von Christa Wolf', *Weimarer Beiträge*, 23 (1977), 110–39.

66. Glossner, Herbert, 'Bunte Reisen aus dem Alltag: Malende Dichterinnen, schreibende Künstler – Sarah Kirsch, Markus Lüpertz und Ursula', *Deutsches Allgemeines Sonntagsblatt*, Reihe Signatur, 3 December 1993.

67. Goheen, Jutta, *et al.*, 'Die Optik der *Zaubersprüche*: Zur Bildpoesie der Sarah Kirsch', *Carleton Germanic Papers*, 9 (1981), 17–40.

68. ——, 'Text als Bild in der Lyrik – besonders von Sarah Kirsch', *Carleton Germanic Papers*, 12 (1984), 51–65.

69. Graves, Peter J. (ed.), *Three Contemporary German Poets: Wolf Biermann, Sarah Kirsch, Reiner Kunze* (Leicester, Leicester University Press, 1985).

70. ——, 'The kite, the plains and some further moralizing', *GDR Monitor*, 19 (1988), 85–90.

71. ——, 'East-West memories of a lost summer: Christa Wolf and Sarah Kirsch', in Arthur Williams, Stuart Parkes, and Roland Smith (eds.), *German Literature at a Time of Change 1989–1990: German Unity and German Identity* (Bern, Peter Lang, 1991), 129–38.

72. ——, 'Sarah Kirsch: some comments and a conversation', *German Life and Letters*, 44 (1991), 271–80.

73. ——, 'Schleswig-Holstein question' [R: *The Brontës Hats, Schwingrasen, Spreu*], *Times Literary Supplement*, 29 May 1992.

74. Grimm, Günter, 'Momentaufnahmen voller Naturmagie und Reiselust: Ein neuer Band mit Gedichten der Lyrikerin Sarah Krisch' [R: *Erlkönigs Tochter*], *Stuttgarter Zeitung*, 30 September 1992.

75. Grützmacher, Curt, 'Sarah Kirsch und Ingo Kühl: *Luft und Wasser*', *Neue Deutsche Hefte*, 35 (1988), 835–6.

76. Guntermann, Georg and Kurzenberger, Hajo, '"Die Nacht streckt ihre Finger aus"', in Peter Bekes *et al.* (eds.), *Deutsche Gegenwartslyrik: Zahlreiche Interpretationen* (Munich, Finck, 1982), 152–60.

77. Günther, Joachim, 'Sarah Kirsch: *Landaufenthalt*', *Neue Deutsche Hefte*, 25 (1978), 346–8.

78. Gutschke, Irmtraud, 'Im Hier-Sein immer ein Anderswo' [R: *Die Flut, Gedichte*], *Neues Deutschland*, 20 July 1990.

79. ——, 'Lyrische Prosa von Sarah Kirsch: Im Schwanengewand', *Neues Deutschland*, 6 December 1991.

80. Hacks, Peter, 'Der Sarah-Sound', *Neue Deutsche Literatur*, 24 No. 9, (1976), 104–18; also in P. Hacks, *Die Maßgaben der Kunst: gesammelte Aufsätze* (Düsseldorf, Classen, 1977), 267–84.

81. Haufs, Rolf, 'Laudatio auf Sarah Kirsch, gehalten am 14. 7. 1983 in Bad Gandersheim anläßlich der Verleihung der Roswitha-Gedenkmedaille', *L'80*, 27 (1983), 166–70.

82. Hartung, Harald, 'Neue Gedichtbücher: Lyrik von Sarah Kirsch, Kay Hoff, Günter Herburger und Rainer Malkowski', *Neue Rundschau*, 88 (1977), 289–95.

83. Heise, Hans-Jürgen, 'Notate aus Matschedonien: Neue Kurzprosa von Sarah Kirsch' [R: *Schwingrasen*], *Stuttgarter Zeitung*, 11 September 1991.

84. Heukenkamp, Ursula, 'Sarah Kirsch: *Zaubersprüche*', *Weimarer Beiträge*, 20 (1974), 150–9.

85. ——, 'Sarah Kirsch: *Die Pantherfrau*', *Weimarer Beiträge*, 21 (1975), 120–33.

86. Hollis, Andy, 'Sarah Kirsch's poem "Der Rest des Fadens": alternative readings', *GDR Monitor*, 6 (1981–82), 40–2.

87. Hulse, Michael, 'Inner emigress: Helga M. Novak and Sarah Kirsch', *The Antigonish Review*, 62–3 (1985), 223–33.

88. Ingen, Ferdinand van, 'Sarah Kirschs *Irrstern*', *Deutsche Bücher*, No. 4 (1986), 265–6.

89. ——, 'Sarah Kirschs *Allerlei-Rauh*', *Deutsche Bücher*, No. 1 (1989), 28–9.

90. Jacobs, Jürgen, 'Elster am Zaum: Ein Prosaband von Sarah Kirsch', *Kölner Stadt-Anzeiger*, 15–16 February 1992.

91. Jakobs, Karl Heinz, '"Du sollst es immer gut haben im Leben": Über Sarah Kirsch', in Annie Voigtländer (ed.), *Liebes- und andere Erklärungen* (Berlin, Weimar, 1972), 167–73.

92. Jauch, Christa, 'Die Pantherfrau', *Deutsch als Fremdsprache*, Sonderheft 14 (1977), 70–2.

93. Jessen, Jens, 'Nachwort', in Sarah Kirsch, *Die ungeheuren bergehohen Wellen auf See*, (Zurich, Manesse, 1987), 91–100.

94. Jendryschik, Manfred, '"Zu Lande zu Wasser"', *Sinn und Form*, 20 (1968), 1247–54.

95. Jones, Calvin N., '"Naturschutzgebiet" von Sarah Kirsch: Gedicht-Interpretation', in *Die Mauersegler* (Aalborg, 1992), 30–2.

96. Kaiser, Joachim, 'Heiter bockige Einsiedlerin: Zweimal Notate von Sarah Kirsch', *Süddeutsche Zeitung*, 16–17 November 1991.

97. ——, 'Kleines Meisterwerk und größere Hoffnung: *Das simple Leben* der Sarah Kirsch' [R], *Beilage Süddeutsche Zeitung*, 63, 111.

98. Kaltwasser, Gerda, '"Man ist viel, wenn man ein Dichter ist": Düsseldorfs Heine-Ehrengabe für Sarah Kirsch', *Rheinische Post*, 14 December 1992.

99. ——, 'Lebensbilder von tätigen Frauen' *Neues Deutschland*, 7 March 1974 [R: *Pantherfrau, Die ungeheuren bergehohen Wellen*].

100. Kaufmann, Hans, 'Zur DDR–Literatur der siebziger Jahre', *Sinn und Form*, 30 (1978), 171–6.

101. Kocsány, Piroska, 'Sarah Kirsch: "Hirtenlied": Versuch einer semantischen Analyse', *Arbeiten zur deutschen Philologie*, 11 (1977), 115–30.

102. ——, 'Skizze zu einer semantischen Analyse lyrischer Texte – veranschaulicht an Gedichten von Sarah Kirsch', *Arbeiten zur deutschen Philologie*, 13 (1979), 253–65.

103. Kunne, Andrea, 'Sarah Kirschs *Katzenleben*', *Deutsche Bücher*, No. 4 (1984), 270–1.

104. Kurz, Paul Konrad, 'Gestörte und wiederhergestellte Idylle', in P. K. Kurz (ed.), *Zwischen Widerstand und Wohlstand: Zur Lyrik der frühen 80er Jahre* (Frankfurt am Main, Knecht, 1986), 167.

105. Kersten, Paul, 'Die Kunst der umherschweifenden Seele: zur Kindheitserfahrung in *Allerlei-Rauh*', *Text + Kritik*, 101 (1989), 69–75.

106. Kirsten, Wulf, '"Die Welt ist ein Gehöft im Winter": Rede auf Sarah Kirsch', *Heine Jahrbuch*, 32 (1993), 172–80.

107. Kolbe, Uwe, 'Verliebt in die berühmte Frau: Zu Sarah Kirschs 60. Geburtstag', *Rheinischer Merkur*, 14 April 1995.

108. Lämmert, Eberhard, 'Stimmenzauber', in *Frankfurter Anthologie*, 2 (Frankfurt am Main, Insel, 1977), 245–8 [on: 'Klosterruine Dschwari'].

109. Leistner, Bernd, '"Mittag und zunehmende Kälte": Sarah Kirsch *Die Flut*' [R], *Neue Deutsche Literatur*, 38 No. 4 (1990), 54.

110. Lenz, Hermann, 'Verwandelte Gartenarbeit', in *Frankfurter Anthologie*, 11 (Frankfurt am Main, Insel, 1988) 242–4 [on: 'Erdreich'].

111. Lermen, Birgit and Loewen, Matthias, 'Sarah Kirsch: Würdigung und Interpretation der drei folgenden Gedichte; "Katzenkopfpflaster", "Der Himmel schuppt sich" und "Tilia Cordata"', in B. Lermen and M. Loewen, *Lyrik aus der DDR: Exemplarische Analysen* (Paderborn, Schöningh, 1987), 315–42.

112. Lermen, Birgit, '"Gefeit machen gegen Verrat und samtige Sprüche": Die Dichterin Sarah Kirsch', *Zeitschrift zur politischen Bildung*, 30 (1993), 104–15.

113. Lersch, Barbara, '"Verschiedene Zeit": Naturerfahrung als reflektiertes Zeitbewußtsein in Sarah Kirschs *Katzenleben*', *Der Deutschunterricht*, 38 (1986), 79–89.

114. Lindquist, Sigvard, 'Sarah Kirsch och värt "sonderfallande hus"', *Horizont*, 38 No. 3 (1991), 8–10 [on: *Allerlei-Rauh*].

115. Loeper, Heidrun, '"Emanzipatzjon" und Kassetten-Recorder', *Neue Deutsche Literatur*, 8 (1974), 144–7 [on: *Pantherfrau, Die ungeheuren bergehohen Wellen*].

116. 'Lyrik in dieser Zeit: Interpretation der Lyrik von Volker Braun, Sarah Kirsch, Axel Schulze und Kito Lorenc, Georg Maurer' [Von einem Kollektiv des Instituts für deutsche Literaturgeschichte der Karl-Marx-Universität Leipzig], *Neue Deutsche Literatur*, 16 (1968), 142–71.

117. Mabee, Barbara, '"Im Totenspiel ungewisser Bedeutung": Antirassistische Assoziationsräume in der Lyrik von Sarah Kirsch', *Jahrbuch zur Literatur in der DDR*, 6 (1987), 143–61.

118. ——, *Die Poetik von Sarah Kirsch: Erinnerungsarbeit und Geschichtsbewußtsein* (Amsterdam, Atlanta, Rodopi, 1989).

119. ——, 'Geschichte, Erinnerung und Zeit: Sarah Kirschs Lyrik', in Ute Brandes (ed.), *Zwischen gestern und morgen: Schriftstellerinnen der DDR aus amerikanischer Sicht* (Bern, Peter Lang, 1992), 221–36.

120. ——, 'Remembrance of the Holocaust in the poetry of Sarah Kirsch', in Elaine Martin (ed.), *Gender, Patriarchy, and Fascism in the Third Reich: The Response of Women Writers* (Detroit, Wayne State University Press, 1993).

121. Maltzan, Carlotta von, '"Man müßte ein Mann sein": Zur Frage der weiblichen Identität in Erzählungen von Kirsch, Morgner und Wolf', *Acta Germanica*, 20 (1990), 141–55.

122. Matt, Peter Von, '*Schwingrasen* und *Spreu*: Die Prosa der Dichterin Sarah Kirsch' [R], *Frankfurter Allgemeine Zeitung*, 8 October 1991.

123. Matz, Wolfgang, 'Wühlmaus unterm Gras: *Das simple Leben*' [R], *Frankfurter Allgemeine Zeitung*, 15 March 1994.

124. Melin, Charlotte, 'Landscape as writing and revelation in Sarah Kirsch's "Death Valley"', *Germanic Review*, 62 (1987), 199–204.

125. Meusinger, Annette, '"ich dacht ich sterbe so fror ich . . . "': Eine Annäherung an die Texte von Sarah Kirsch', in Ulrich Kaufmann (ed.), *Verbannt und Verkannt* (Jena, Saale, 1992), 84–95.

126. Michaelis, Rolf, '"Nichtmehr und Nochnicht": Zwei neue Bücher von Sarah Kirsch; Der Prosaband *Schwingrasen* und das Bilder-Tagebuch *Spreu*', *Die Zeit*, 18 October 1991.

127. Mierau, Fritz, 'Novella Mateeva und Sarah Kirsch', in *Konturen und Perspektiven* (Berlin, Akademie, 1969), 69–80.

128. Mohr, Heinrich, 'Die Lust "Ich" zu sagen: Versuch über die Lyrik der Sarah Kirsch', in Lothar Jordan, Axel Marquardt and Winfried Woesler (eds.), *Lyrik – von allen Seiten* (Frankfurt am Main, Fischer, 1981), 439–60.

129. Mohr, Peter, 'Tiefenstromung "haut uns die Füße weg": Prosa von Sarah Kirsch in dem Band *Das simple Leben*' [R], *Rheinische Post*, 16 April 1994.

130. ——, 'Mensch und Natur: Zum 60. Geburtstag der Lyrikerin Sarah Kirsch', *Berliner Zeitung*, Easter 1995.

131. Neumann, Walter and Juhre, Arnim, 'Sie läßt die Feder fliegen: *Spreu* und *Schwingrasen*: Tagebuchaufzeichnungen von Sarah Kirsch. Erinnerungen an die DDR, norddeutsche Impressionen' [R], *Deutsches Allgemeines Sonntagsblatt*, 17 January 1992.

132. Nissen, Klaus, 'Bürger und Flüchtlinge lauschten Sarah: Frankfurter Verlagsinitiative gegen Gewalt und Fremdenhaß hatte Lesung ermöglicht', *Frankfurter Rundschau*, 16 November 1992.

133. Opelt, Edith, 'Sprache über den Augenblick hinaus: *Unfrisierte Erzählungen aus dem Kassetten-Recorder* von Sarah Kirsch', *Neue Zeit*, 27 April 1974.

134. Politzer, Heinz, 'Verhohlene Leidenschaft als politische Metapher', in *Frankfurter Anthologie*, 3 (Frankfurt am Main, Insel, 1978), 254–6 [on: 'Nachricht aus Lesbos'].

135. Post, Laura, 'The poetry of Sarah Kirsch', in *The Rackham Journal of the Arts and Humanities* (Ann Arbor, 1986), 81–94.

136. Pulver, Elspeth, 'Ein sehr schöner Traum voller Arbeit: *Schwingrasen* – Prosa von Sarah Kirsch' [R], *Neue Zürcher Zeitung*, 18 September 1992.

137. Raddatz, Fritz J., 'Eine neue Subjektivität formt neue Realität', in F. J. Raddatz, *Traditionen und Tendenzen. Materialen zur Literatur der DDR* (Frankfurt am Main, Suhrkamp, 1972), 167–73.

138. Radisch, Iris, 'Siebenmeilenstiefelchen: Sarah Kirschs Gedichtband *Erlkönigs Tochter*', *Die Zeit*, 4 December 1992.

139. Radisch, Iris, 'Deutschdeutsches Gewese Notizen vom Tage: Andreas Neumeister, Christa Wolf und Sarah Kirsch. Ein Gespräch, das nicht stattfindet', *Die Zeit*, 18 March 1994.

140. Reich-Ranicki, Marcel, 'Der Droste jüngere Schwester: Über die Lyrik der Sarah Kirsch', in M. Reich-Ranicki, *Entgegnungen* (Stuttgart, Deutsche Verlags-Anstalt, 1981), 219–32.

141. Reinacher, Pia, 'Lyrisierende Prosa: zu Sarah Kirschs *Schwingrasen*', *Schweizer Monatshefte*, 72 (1992), 342–4.

142. Riha, Karl, 'Rezidivierende Naturlyrik – oder: zu Sarah Kirschs *Katzenleben*', *Text + Kritik*, 101 (1989), 46–51.

143. ——, 'Lyrik im Eiswind: zu Sarah Kirschs *Schneewärme*', *Diagonal*, 2 (1991), 173–5.

144. Rothmann, Kurt, 'Sarah Kirsch', in K. Rothmann, *Deutschsprachige Schriftsteller seit 1945: Einzeldarstellungen* (Stuttgart, Reclam, 1985), 223–6.

145. Rühle, J., 'Kein Platz für Poesie: Sarah Kirsch', *Deutschland-Archiv*, 9 (1977), 897–8.

146. Schacht, Ulrich, 'Auf der Flucht vor der Geschichte: Christa Wolfs Selbstoffenbarung in *Reden, Briefen und Aufsätzen seit der Wende*; Sarah Kirschs melancholisches Werkstatt-Tagebuch' [R], *Die Welt*, 17 March 1994.

147. Schädlich, Hans Joachim, 'Die Spreu und der Weizen: Sarah Kirschs Notizen von ihren Lesereisen', *Der Tagesspiegel*, 15 September 91.

148. Schneider, Rolf, 'Zwischen Aufgang und Untergang', *Frankfurter Anthologie*, 3 (Frankfurt am Main, Insel, 1978), 250–2.

149. Schulz, Gerhard, 'Ohne Heimweh', *Frankfurter Anthologie*, 10 (Frankfurt am Main, Insel, 1986), 248–50.

150. Schulte, Bettina, 'Sarah Kirsch empfing in Staufen den Huchel-Preis', *Badische Zeitung*, 5 April 1993.

151. Schwarz, Peter Paul, 'Gleichzeitigkeit als dichterisches Verfahren: Zu Sarah Kirschs Gedichtband *Landaufenthalt*', *Neue Deutsche Hefte*, 35 (1988), 239–55.

152. Seehafer, Klaus, '*Rückenwind*', *Neue Deutsche Hefte*, 24 (1977), 357–9.

153. Seibt, Ursula, 'Sarah Kirsch . . . , "viele Dinge hindern uns Menschen"', *Buchhändler heute*, 2 (1979), 95–7.

154. Serke, Jürgen, '"Wir haben die DDR als Irrenanstalt erlebt": Gespräch mit Sarah Kirsch und Ulrich Zieger', *Die Welt*, 16 December 1991.

155. ———, 'Das Frührot des Zweiten Tages: Zu Gast bei Sarah Kirsch in der Landschaft ihrer Natur', *Die Welt*, 7 September 1991.

156. ———, 'Eine Arche als Zirkuswagen: Sarah Kirschs Antwort auf die Weltenwende', *Die Weltwoche*, 31 March 1994.

157. Shaw, Peter, 'The significance of the kite above the plains: a thorough interpretation of Sarah Kirsch's poem 'Der Rest des Fadens', *GDR Monitor*, 17 (1987), 48–63.

158. Skulski, Gudrun, 'Im Spiegel eigenen Empfindens: Begegnungen mit der Schriftstellerin Sarah Kirsch', *Neue Zeit*, 21 December 1974.

159. Sperr, Franziska, 'Von der Schwierigkeit, die Balance zu halten: Ein Brief und seine Folgen', *L'80*, 14 (1980), 130–3.

160. Spiel, Hilde, 'Laudatio auf Sarah Kirsch', *Literatur und Kritik*, 153 (1981), 132–6.

161. Stoljar, Margaret, 'Das Ende der Utopie: Kunert und Kirsch als Modelle einer neuen Exilliteratur', in David Roberts (ed.), *Tendenzwenden: Aspekte des Kulturwandels der 70er Jahre* (Frankfurt am Main, Peter Lang, 1984), 163–82.

162. Terras, R., '*Erlkönigs Tochter*', *World Literature Today*, 62 No. 2 (1993), 378–8.

163. Törne, Dorothea von, '"Balance auf dem Messer": Sarah Kirsch rettet sich in die Figur des Robinson', *Der Tagesspiegel*, 30 April–1 May 1995.

164. Töteberg, Michael, 'Literatur aus dem Kassetten-Recorder? Kontexte zu Sarah Kirschs Erzählungsband *Die Pantherfrau*', *Text + Kritik*, 101 (1989), 82–9.

165. Totten, Monika 'Alltagsgeschichte in Dialog: DDR-Protokoll-Literatur von Frauen', in Ute Brandes (ed.), *Zwischen gestern und morgen: Schriftstellerinnen der DDR aus amerikanischer Sicht* (Bern, Peter Lang, 1992), 42–54 [on: *Die Pantherfrau*].

166. Treichel, Hans-Ulrich, 'Wo der Schwingrasen die Füße feucht hält: Sarah Kirschs lyrische Prosa aus Holstein', *Der Tagesspiegel*, 9 October 1991.

167. ——, 'Das fremde furchtbare Blick: Sarah Kirschs neue Prosa über das vermeintlich simple Leben' [R], *Der Tagesspiegel*, 26 June 1994.

168. Uecker, Kari, 'Tre klarsynte kvinner: Christa Wolf, Irmtraud Morgner, Sarah Kirsch', *Vinduet*, 37 (1983), 35–9.

169. Volckmann, Silvia, *Zeit der Kirschen? Das Naturbild in der deutschen Gegenwartslyrik: Jürgen Becker, Sarah Kirsch, Wolf Biermann, Hans Magnus Enzensberger* (Königstein, Forum Academicum, Athenäum, 1982).

170. Wagener, Hans, *Sarah Kirsch* [*Köpfe des 20. Jahrhunderts*], vol. 113 (Berlin, Kolloquium, 1989).

171. Wallace, Ian, 'Überlegungen zu *Erdreich*', in I. Wallace (ed.), *GDR in the 1980s* (Dundee, GDR Monitor, 1984), 121–33.

172. Wallmann, Jürgen P., 'Anspruch auf ein volles Leben', *Deutschland-Archiv*, 12 (1974), 1315–18.

173. ——, 'Ich gedenke nicht am Heimweh zu sterben', *Deutschland-Archiv*, 15 (1982), 984–6 [R: *Erdreich*].

174. ——, 'Naturpoesie: Sarah Kirsch *Katzenleben*', *Deutschland-Archiv*, 17 (1984), 1338–9.

175. Wallmann, Jürgen P., 'Arme Landschaft – reiche Sprache', *Literatur und Kritik* [R: *Irrstern*], 209/10 (1986), 469–71; also in *Neue Deutsche Hefte*, 34 (1987), 159–62; first appeared in *Der Tagespiegel*, 24 August 1986.

176. ——, 'Gefeit gegen samtige Sprüche: nach zwei Prosawerken folgt jetzt wieder ein neuer Lyrikband von Sarah Kirsch', *Rheinischer Merkur*, 2 October 1992.

177. ——, 'Poetischer Sog der vier Welt-Enden' [R: *Ich Crusoe*], *Rheinische Post*, 15 April 95.

178. Weinrich, Harald, 'Langsam gelesen', in *Frankfurter Anthologie 4*, (Franfkurt am Main, Insel, 1979), 24–244 [on: 'Einäugig'].

179. Wernhauser, Richard, 'Sarah Kirsch: *Katzenleben*', *Neue Deutsche Hefte*, 31 (1984), 366–8.

180. Westphal, Anke, 'Fremder Blick nach draußen: Sarah Kirsch zwischen Landidylle und Weltpolitik', *Berliner Zeitung*, 6 June 1994.

181. ——, 'Hinter den sieben Deichen lebt Sarah Kirsch zwischen Landidylle und Weltpolitik', *die tageszeitung*, 11 June 1994.

182. Widmer, Urs, 'Sarah Kirsch ist eine Hexe', *Neue Literatur*, 27 No. 9 (1976), 67–8.

183. Wiegenstein, Roland H., 'Sarah Kirsch – approbierte Hexe, Sprechstunden nach Vereinbarung', *Merkur*, 31 (1977), 78–84.

184. Wittkowski, Wolfgang, 'Sarah Kirsch', in Klaus Weissenberger (ed.), *Die deutsche Lyrik 1945–1975* (Düsseldorf, Bagel, 1981), 366–72.

185. Wittkowski, Wolfgang, 'Sarah Kirsch: "Der Milchmann Schäuffele"', *German Quarterly*, 54 (1981), 311–17.

186. ——, *Andeuten und Verschleiern in Dichtungen von Plautus bis Hemingway und von der Goethezeit bis Sarah Kirsch* (Frankfurt am Main, Peter Lang, 1993).

187. Wolf-Gentile, Marga, 'La poésie de Sarah Kirsch au passage des frontières', *Etudes Germaniques*, 25 (1993), 199–205.

188. Wolf, Gerhard, 'Ausschweifungen und Verwünschungen. Vorläufige Bemerkungen zu Motiven bei Sarah Kirsch', *Text + Kritik*, 101 (1989), 13–28.

189. Zimmermann, Harro, 'Im Metrum des Windes: Sarah Kirschs Prosaband *Schwingrasen*', *Frankfurter Rundschau*, 9 October 1991.

Index